The Birth of Savitṛ

The Birth of Savitṛ

A Poetic Composition based on
Sri Aurobindo's *Savitri*

R Y Deshpande

The Sri Aurobindo Center of Los Angeles
The East-West Cultural Center
Los Angeles
U.S.A.

First Published
21 February 2003

Cover Design
Arun Mohanty

Published by
The Sri Aurobindo Center of Los Angeles
The East-West Cultural Center
12329 Marshall Street, Culver City, CA. 90230
U.S.A.
Phone: (310) 390-9083;
Fax: (310) 390-7763;
Email: ewcc@earthlink.net
Website: http://www.sriaurobindocenter-la.org

ISBN: 0–930736–04–4

Price (Soft Cover)
Rs.   100.00 (India)
US$ 7.00 (Overseas)

Phototypeset and Printed at
All India Press
Kennedy Nagar
Pondicherry 605 001
India

Contents

Author's Note

If we are looking for the Word that brings to us the dynamic Divine, our rush is towards Sri Aurobindo's *Savitri*. It gives us the Truth and the things of the Truth and in it is our soul's completest fulfilment. Therefore all that we achieve we truly owe to *Savitri*.

A year ago I would have least imagined that I would be writing short compositions based on each canto of *Savitri*. But on 22 March 2002 I received from William Netter a copy of his work entitled *Savitrima*. This is basically an endeavour to present the metaphysical core of *Savitri*. The book is an informal production and my copy is 11 of 49. With a canto on each right page, and the Mother's eyes looking into ours, we actually have here *Savitri in 20 Minutes*. I read it a number of times, back and forth, and had initially some mixed feelings about the whole attempt. Yet an inscrutable seed was cast and in less than a month's time it started sprouting and growing.

Soon the work was completed, on 5 June 2002, and I gave one printout to Amal Kiran, the grand old man of the Aurobindonian world of poetry. His generous compliments were a heartening encouragement to me and I began to have confidence in my enterprise. In fact I must recall that my own poetic apprenticeship had begun under him about fifty years ago and I am very happy that his guidance has been available to me throughout.

A number of *Savitri*-lovers and experts here around have gone through the "cantos" and I am sincerely thankful to them all. I would particularly like to mention the names of Jugal Kishore Mukherji, Georges van Vrekhem, Shyam Sunder Jhunjhunwala, Asoka K. Ganguli, Ravi, and Richard Hartz. One of my friends suggested that for the benefit of a general reader, who has not always the right resources at his disposal, I must provide the relevant material. Although the addition of a few prose sections to take care of this aspect makes the book of poems somewhat odd, I thought it worthwhile in the context of *Savitri*.

As a very special note of appreciation I must say a few words about Debashish Banerji of the East-West Cultural Center at Los Angeles. When I sent the "cantos" to him as an e-mail attachment I had requested him to go through them carefully and offer his comments and corrections. And indeed he did, canto-by-canto and line-by-line, checking even the punctuation marks. His suggestions were especially valuable to me and I have taken note of them suitably while giving the second reading to the work. He was so much impressed by it that he even put it on the Center's website. When requested he agreed without any reservation to write the foreword in spite of his other packed occupations.

I consider it to be a great honour that the Los Angeles Center should have come forward to bring out *The Birth of Savitṛ* as an aspect of literary and cultural promotion. My special thanks are due to the members of the board.

My young friend Arun Mohanty worked enthusiastically and tirelessly in designing the cover for the book. To another young friend, Ashika Sharma, goes the credit of doing the title of the book in a calligraphic style based on Sri Aurobindo's handwriting. This has been used on page 1. My fond appreciation for all that they did with care and devotion.

Invocation to Savitṛ

तत्सवितुर्वरं रूपं ज्योतिः परस्य
धीमहि ।
यन्नः सत्येन दीपयेत् ॥

tat savitur varam rūpam jyotiḥ parasya dhīmahi |
yannaḥ satyena dīpayet ||

*Let us meditate on the most
auspicious (best) form of Savitri,
on the Light of the Supreme
which shall illumine us with
the Truth.*

Let us meditate on the most auspicious (best) form of Savitri,
the Light of the Supreme
which shall illumine us with the Truth.

The invocation in Sri Aurobindo's Gayatri Mantra in Sanskrit is to the
Sun-God Savitṛ; accordingly in its English rendering the word *Savitri*
should be read in that context. We celebrate the Birth of Savitṛ—the
Sun-God in the present composition based on Sri Aurobindo's *Sāvitrī*.

She is Savitri

Incarnate in the beauty and joy of the Rose,
Fulfilling the Infinite in the perfect form,
Bringing to the heart of Time the Eternal,
Like a dawn borne by the chariot of the sun
To our day giving the vast of the Truth-Light,
She has come in the mystery of her love.
Goldening the tassel, purpling the fringe,
She is the honey-brightness of the flower,
And awakes the sleep and ennobles the vilest things;
She has cut the knot of the mountains with her sword,
And with the gaze of her eyes kindled the bagatelle,
And from the sky of her being poured delight.
Her flame is the Will of the High burning in the Dark,
And her name is seventy-million hymns:
She is Savitri, the daughter of the Unborn,
And in her coming is the advent of God's hour.

7 February 1985

To Her

Born from the fire of heaven and kindled on earth
Her flame was set ablaze in the darkness's breast;
A power was in her that knew no defeat,
Yet her joy beautiful like the moonlit night,
The soul of a goddess in the body of time,
A tranquil ocean flowing in a glad stream.
She wore like a robe pink of the infinite
And walked a future's figure to change destiny,
To chastise the spirit of death with deathless love.
World after world she went twelve occult times out
And broke the seal that lay on the mantra of life,—
And in a sudden chant arose the splendid sun.

18 August 2002

Foreword

A long poem called *The Birth of Savitṛ*, which seems in some way, an attempt to encapsulate Sri Aurobindo's cosmic epic *Savitri* – is this not an irrelevant if not sacrosanct gesture? Since *Savitri* is already couched in the suggestive translucencies of overmental poetry, what utility is there in diminishing, quantitatively and qualitatively the supreme original? Is it not to render more obscure the already obscure? And considering the gathering religiosity around the epic, is it not impolitic, a dangerous heresy?

In his extended apologia, R.Y. Deshpande tries to answer, from the author's vantage, some of these questions which may arise naturally in the mind of the prospective reader of this book. He goes to some length to express his awareness of the futility of trying to encompass the infinite epic, reproduce its poetic zenith, rewrite the avatars' double autobiography or shape a word vessel for the divine consciousness and clearly disavows these as his intentions. He then proceeds to indicate what he considers to be a true and bountiful relation which any reader may have with the extraordinary epic, word embodiment of the supramental grace-light, not only in consciousness but in expression. In his words: *What is necessary is that we should just contemplatively live in her gleaming ambiance. This also means that there are as many ways of living in her glad presence as are the individuals who approach her with an urge to find the true spirit of divinity in every thing, material as well as heavenly. One could do meditative paintings, or compose new musical opuses, or present her in operatic magnificence, or sculpt her moods of love and laughter, or speak of her in participative discourses, or write hymns and poems in praise of her, or in deep choreographic gestures bring her movements to the world of men and matter. And if it is a creative effort then each composition will carry in it the soul of the particular artist himself. Each one will then have his own* Savitri, *each sculptor a bust of his own goddess, each doer of yogic tapasya a characteristic aura of hers.* In this light, he clarifies what he sees as the just character of his poem: *We may call these cantos as brief meditations on* Savitri.

Therefore they are entirely subjective in character. Elsewhere, in his introduction to the second collection of essays on *Savitri, Perspectives of Savitri II*, which he has recently edited – adapting an image from the Maharashtran saint-poet Jnaneshwar, he has expressed it more imaginatively: *we are like a bird that can hardly hold in its beak any quantity of the water of a vast sunlit lake by whose side it builds its tiny nest. Yet whatever is there in that little bird's bill is that lake's own wonderment. Such only can be the glad merit of a collection of works being presented in two volumes with some fifty and odd articles in it.*[1] Relative to the form of expression, I may add that to live saturated with the music of the spheres at the originary source of its fountain of inspiration, what could be more natural, if one has the capacity, than to open to the divine Muse and bear in oneself the passage of her poetic word?

But are all such expressions worthy? Justifications we may provide for all manner of personal expression based on authentic relationship with the resplendent epic-goddess, but are we not accountable to some standards; and if so, what may these be? Cultural relativism has today hazed the issue of aesthetic standards, so that to some it seems politically incorrect even to mention the existence of any such thing. But to the followers of Sri Aurobindo and the Mother, the Sun of Beauty is among the absolutes of the supramental existence and draws our expressions magnetically towards its height. The circumstances from which these rise, the stylistic precedents they draw from or the raw materials or technologies which they command may be vastly different, but the development of an increasing intuition of and receptivity to spiritual sublimity in its varied forms is a necessary consequence of an integral growth into the spirit and dictates its own standards. Moreover, the legacy of the Mother and Sri Aurobindo is a rich body of pointers opening the way to the cultural standards of the future, not rigid commandments but recognizable in consciousness; and it remains for us to embody the states in our lives and work which would make these standards living and manifest. To aspire sincerely to reach the aesthetic heights described and revealed by

---

[1] Ed. R.Y. Deshpande, *Perspectives of Savitri II*, Pondicherry, 2002, lxiv.

Them, to recognize future expectations and exceed the present in manifesting them, is as necessary for us in expression as it is in consciousness, if we are to be integrally true to the Mother's creative *shakti*. In this, the form of art which has received, undoubtedly, the clearest elucidation is Poetry (specifically English), where Sri Aurobindo has given us both a theory of the mantra in *The Future Poetry* and ample heuristic leads to its practice in his letters on the subject. However, this theory and these leads are hardly obvious to those who have not aspired to make them realities in intuition and experience. (And as a corollary, the absence or paucity of such elaboration in other art forms is no excuse for the disregard of comparable standards in these cases.) Sri Aurobindo himself saw *Savitri* less as a poem to be finished than an attempt to sustain the unalloyed expression of the overmental mantra in the English language. To this effect, he recast innumerably, particularly the first canto so that there may be in it no mixture, all in it may come from the same and highest mint. To be thus impersonal to one's expression and to be conscious of some peak intuition of spiritual quality in one's striving can be identified as key elements in doing the works of creativity in the Integral Yoga. Deshpande is amply conscious of this, though he states his expectations with modesty: *its tendency to become inner mental, though perhaps at times touched by the overhead, will dominate.* The overhead touch is achieved far more frequently in the present work than "perhaps at times", according to me, justifying not merely the right to sing, but the worthiness, in terms of a rare contemporary advance towards the future poetry. It stands as an example of those shining standards set by the Master, which few today have had the courage or conviction to attempt, much less to realize.

The *tendency to become inner mental,* which the author cautiously announces as a probable property of his poem, is seen by him as consequence of the constrained discipline he has imposed on himself. This discipline, which determines the poem's form, is a deliberate restriction of each canto of his poem to a twelve line subjective condensation of the corresponding canto from *Savitri*. Recently, a similar radical compression has been attempted of that other magnum opus of Sri Aurobindo, *The Life Divine*. I am referring to G.R. Sarma's *The Life Divine – A Brief Outline,*[2] which I have reviewed for the SABDA newsletter and for *Jyoti* (Volume IV, Issue 1), the online journal of the Sri Aurobindo Center of Los Angeles. Each sentence (or line) from these two works lends itself to extensive elaboration and several have been the attempts made in the past by considerable stalwarts, such as A.B. Purani, Madhav Pandit and others, to introduce the densities of these works to a lay public through elaboration. The attempt is necessary and continues. But I must admit the sense of disappointment that has inevitably accompanied my readings of such attempts, and for no want of understanding, inspiration or eloquence in their authors. On analysis, I realize that this disappointment has been based not merely on the yawning chasm dividing human descriptions, however great, from the power of Sri Aurobindo's writing – such a comparison would be unjust in the extreme – but due exactly to what the authors have attempted, the banality of simplification. The necessary drop of consciousness to the "common light of earthly day" robs Sri Aurobindo's lines of their holographic multi-dimensionality and renders them flat. The sense of pacing, like Aswapati, through the vast cathedral of Sri Aurobindo's Thought, "under its arches dim with infinity",[3] is replaced by the glinting clarities of rational understanding. By choosing a direction the opposite of elaboration, Sarma and Deshpande initiate a new trend, one of attempting to concentrate in their work the *tapas-shakti* of the original instead of dissipating it. Whether this renders the original more accessible, in what ways and to whom are moot questions, resting for their answers on the specifics of method. In both cases, a graspable silhouette is sought, a linked unity, a glimpse of essential form and proportion. In Deshpande's case, by using poetry to address the poetic body of *Savitri*, a refreshing gain is the greater preservation of suggestive ambiguity, a sense of the infinite reservoir that not only the epic but each line in it is. Deshpande is, in fact, very conscious of the overwhelming cosmic quality of *Savitri*'s lines and the diminution of amplitude that is likely to result from his

---

[2] G.N. Sarma, *Sri Aurobindo — The Life Divine : A Brief Outline,* Bangalore, 2001.
[3] Sri Aurobindo, *Savitri,* Pondicherry, 1993, p. 79.

self-imposed constraint. This in fact is what draws from him his already quoted comment regarding his personal expectation of quality in his poem: *its tendency to become inner mental, though perhaps at times touched by the overhead, will dominate.* However, he is also well aware of the promise contained in his approach and this is what draws him to the venture. About this reward he says: *Yet possibly it could secure in its deep hushful seed-state everything.*

What could he mean by this? In my review of Sarma's outline of *The Life Divine*, I tried to enumerate the forms of miniaturization in art and place Sarma's work within this classification. The four varieties of miniature representation I identified there can be summarized as (1) photographic reduction; (2) impressionism; (3) expressionism; and (4) minimalism. Neither Sarma's work nor Deshpande's claims to be photographic reduction. In Sarma's case, I identified his outline as aspiring to a condition of pure minimalism – an attempt to arrive at what he considers the bare bones of each chapter of *The Life Divine*, its logical skeleton. While this may be attempted for philosophy, *Savitri* can hardly be seen as primarily an edifice of structured ideas. Yet there is a structure, a plot, an inexorable progression to it and in compressing each canto into twelve lines, Deshpande certainly has his eye on bringing this into bolder relief. In this respect, his work is minimalistic. But what of its evocations? Poetry, after all, cannot but fill outline with suggestion and ornamentation, plot with episodic density. Impressionistic miniaturization brings to a clear focus selected elements of the original that stand out, detailing these, while hazing the rest into background washes. Expressionistic reduction on the other hand, exaggerates and distorts elements and emphases of the original under powerful personal affect. In Far Eastern art, where landscape painting has been taken for centuries as creative representation of nature, many a master has sought a balance between the impressionistic and the expressionistic, between personal expression and impersonal intuitive discovery of essential line, colour and texture. Deshpande's attempt is such a balance – it attempts an accurate subjective impression of each canto but through a personal retelling, using a focused mystic style. Bringing to this the aspiration for the overhead word, his poem becomes a seeking for the *mantra* – a *mantra* that will capture the heart of the grand *mantra* that is *Savitri,* in other words, *Savitri*'s *bija.* This is what he means by *secure[ing] in its...seed-state everything.* In this he succeeds eminently, I believe. Here is no claim for an absolute *bija,* but an authentic personal *bija* of *Savitri* nevertheless, which the author is gifting to us in this poem, and I am grateful to him and to Savitri, the goddess of his inspiration, for it.

DEBASHISH BANERJI

The Sri Aurobindo Center of Los Angeles
The East-West Cultural Center
Los Angeles
U.S.A.

An Apologia

Here is an attempt to present Sri Aurobindo's epic *Savitri* in brief stanza-like cantos each with just twelve lines. *Savitri* is a poem written in pentametric blank verse form, mostly with end-stopped lines, running almost to twenty-four thousand in number. Divided into twelve books, as was the tradition for a classical epic, it has forty-eight cantos plus an epilogue. Part I consisting of the first twenty-four cantos was published in September 1950, just a couple of months before Sri Aurobindo's passing away in December of that year; Part II and Part III as a single tome comprising of the remaining twenty-four cantos and the epilogue appeared in May 1951. The poet spent a number of years in completing the composition, more than thirty years though with some long gaps in between. He also took *Savitri* as a means of ascension in poetic creation towards a higher and more perfect truth experienced by him spiritually. It is an expression of the realized sovereignty itself and hence becomes most valuable. Even in its outward character it is encyclopaedic. Therefore to think of putting such a work in scarcely six hundred lines is a perilous task, fully loaded with the question if this should be done at all. The comprehensive epic possesses simultaneously several dimensions and yet moves through region after luminous region with remarkable swiftness. Also, it was planned and executed with great artistic care, with the essential "power of architectural construction." So to compress it by a factor of forty is to tell stories, if not desecrate the magnificence of its structural design. More serious objection will be the want of spiritual authenticity when we are not in touch with the truth of inspiration behind it. It will be presumptuous on our part even to speak of fidelity to the text charged as it is with yogic experiences.

Sri Aurobindo considered *Savitri* as his main work in the context of his great avataric objective. It is not only the record of a seeing, but is also a supreme revelation of his evolutionary vision and its realization. In its literary aspect it is the Vedic word or the mantra itself. It is "the voice of the rhythm which has created the worlds." Its supremacy is such that it becomes a happy chariot speeding the

Rishi on the ascending slopes of heaven. It could also become a vehicle of awareness and fulfilment for the seeker-souls in their quest towards the great truth, *mahadsatyam*. About it Sri Aurobindo says that it is a word of power born out of the secret depths of our being and is brooded upon by a deeper consciousness. In it one has the sense of a rhythm coming from infinity and rushing to infinity, a rhythm which "has for ever been sounding in the eternal planes and began even in time ages ago and which returns into the infinite to go sounding on for ages after." That is precisely the character of *Savitri*'s word. That is how *Savitri* becomes a creation of the dynamic truth. Therefore, rendering it in any other language or in any other form is possible only if one can go to the very original source which is the creative hush of omniscience. For that to happen one has to dwell in the calm womb of eternity and grow in its summer day. Indeed, its birth is in the Tapas-Shakti and its growth in the action that can bring felicitous prosperity. To discover *Savitri* is to transform our mortality.

If we have to characterize Sri Aurobindo's *Savitri* by suitable epithets, we may very well go to Vyasa's tale in the Mahabharata and use his descriptions of Aswapati's daughter Savitri. She is a radiant daughter, *kanyā tejasvinī*, she is a damsel of heaven, *devakanyā*, she is heavenly and radiant in form, *devarūpiṇī*; she is Goddess Fortune and one who brings the wealth of auspicious gladness, is beautiful and charming, and is also an adept in the esoteric Yoga of Meditation, *dhyānayogaparāyaṇā*, thus equipped to accomplish the purpose for which she has taken this mortal birth in the world of men. Only a supreme King-Yogi can hence bring about amongst us the birth of such a flaming rapturous princess. Such too is the poem. *Savitri* is Sri Aurobindo's daughter. Not only that. When he left his body, he left his consciousness behind forever in it. Indeed, it becomes his spiritual autobiography. Presenting *Savitri* in any other form would then naturally mean writing a quick biography and writing a biography is always a hazardous business, full of shortcomings, generally carrying with it one's own prejudices and preferences, one's own deep-rooted traditions or *samkāras*, and for sure one's own hundred limitations.

It will be therefore wrong to compare a biography with an autobiography,—simply because one is an authentic account and the other, by and large, a derived enterprise even if it were an exceptional achievement. Yet an affable biography with sufficient insight can provide a certain peep into the original and bring yet another perspective of vision. Perhaps that could be its precious gain. After all, *Savitri* should not be treated as a distant unapproachable goddess, staying all of her own in a secluded world of splendour and of calm. She will be of no use then and the undertaking Sri Aurobindo had taken would lose all the relevance for us, for whom he attempted all and achieved all. She is not there to be ritualistically worshipped with flower and fruit and leaf, waved with a burning lamp. What is necessary is that we should just contemplatively live in her gleaming ambiance.

This also means that there are as many ways of living in her glad presence as are the individuals who approach her with an urge to find the true spirit of divinity in every thing, material as well as heavenly. One could do meditative paintings, or compose new musical opuses, or present her in operatic magnificence, or sculpt her moods of love and laughter, or speak of her in participative discourses, or write hymns and poems in praise of her, or in deep choreographic gestures bring her movements to the world of men and matter. And if it is a creative effort then each composition will carry in it the soul of the particular artist himself. Each one will then have his own *Savitri*, each sculptor a bust of his own goddess, each doer of yogic tapasya a characteristic aura of hers. Therefore what we are having here is just one piece of art in a poetic form, suggesting that there will follow many more in the course of spiritually vibrant times. We may call these cantos as brief meditations on *Savitri*. Therefore they are entirely subjective in character.

Any representation of a revelatory creation such as *Savitri* has to face problems of several kind—literary as well as mystic-spiritual. What I have done here is to allot for myself just a dozen lines for each canto of the magnum opus. Sometimes it amounts to speaking of hundreds of lines in merely a few! How atrocious! But the idea is only to indicate, in a suggestive and compressed phrase, the thematic nature of the text which has the canvas of the whole blue firmament to paint the glories of the Sublime. This approach may appear to be a sort of forced or artificial way of doing things, but perhaps it has also an advantage in stating the premise in a brief manner. This must mean that, for a reader steeped in *Savitri*, these pieces would appear too sketchy without the Rasa of the sweet and melodious expansive mood of the original. On the other hand, for a beginner not acquainted with the Master's epic things will come with incoherent painful jolts and the smooth essay-like continuity that readily carries him along may be missing.

These contemplations on each canto of *Savitri* under the title *The Birth of Savitr —the Sun-God* could have as well been collected in a volume bearing the name *The Book of Savitri*. This would have maintained a direct connection with the original, implying that the composition was an attempt to provide in a poetic form a compacted argument of each canto of the epic. We have precedence available to us, albeit in prose, in Milton's *Paradise Lost* where the books have at the beginning the thematic substance of what is going to follow in the respective text. The advantage is that the reader is at once provided with a certain desirable conceptual support making his movements aesthetically steady and definite. This certainly helps him grasp the sequence that runs invisibly through the literary stateliness of the narrative. In fact, when the main line of reasoning is thus established the story so formed itself becomes an artistic creation. Can a similar undertaking, be it in prose or poetry, have any acceptability for the spiritual poem which *Savitri* is? Can meditations be taken as arguments?

But then this would amount to intellectualizing what must really be felt intuitively and the plain answer would be 'No'. Howsoever genuine the effort be, whatever mystery and music the poems may possess, even if one may derive pleasure from them, or stand rather a-gape looking at them as mini-wonders, or savour the new and strange preparations, or offer pleased silence in their appreciation, one ought to immediately experience some unfaltering quality of inspiration behind them. In their compacted thematic presentation they may seem pretty well digested and the heavenly Muse might have even pressed her sparkly or miraculous feet on several lines and made a concrete impression; yet the streaming joy in its sweet tranquil enthusiasm, in its enchanting rush that creates the original would be missing. Sri Aurobindo himself says that *Savitri* renders into poetry a symbol of things occult and spiritual. In fact it has the essence of a universal consciousness which brings with it wide and luminous knowledge, power, charm, beauty in possession of the truth and truth in the lure of beauty, and the obligation is that these must at least in some degree be present in any other creation of it. Will it be then legitimate to redo the Great Ashwattha Tree in any other form? This redoing may belong to music or painting or poetry or gardening such as the Japanese bonsai. But whatever be the mode it is to be well understood that this kingly Tree has its glowing roots in the soil of the upper sky and its luxurious branches spread down below. Naturally, therefore, howsoever perfectly it be crafted and with whatever care tended, the bonsai can never hold the kingly distinction and all that one can expect to happen is the appearance of a greenish shade of its celestial verdure in our scheduled life. An indistinct or faint note of its existence's delight is all that we may at times be able to hear in the hassle and scurry of our daily rounds.

Yet I suppose this composition has its own worth and its own appeal, its own good point, perhaps holding a keenness of another aesthetic denomination, another possibility of perceptive enjoyment. Firstly, we cannot have the epic style for short compositions as are presented here. The technique I have adopted is mostly that of a short even narrative, though at times it may be lyric-sensitive or occult-symbolical. In the process there is the likelihood of moving far away from the original's wholesome Hellenistic beauty and of falling into the trimmed expressive form that is profiled and geometric in character. The visual and tactile creativity may then seem to recede, leaving behind only the sharp cyberic. Which means that the snippety nature with its tendency to become inner mental, though perhaps at times touched by the overhead, will dominate. Yet possibly it could secure in its deep hushful seed-state everything.

But if due care is not taken the result could be disastrous also. Growing bonsai is always a delicate affair. In the objectionable act of poetic thematization one may end up with something that will be far removed from the author's actual intent. The whole exercise of expressing *Savitri* in brief cantos may finally just arrive at some vague and dubious turn of phrases with "mystic sense, cryptic quintessence, or gnomic gist", if not fuddled compression taking the place of what should be vivid and spontaneous and gracefully fluent. "Oh, this brave attempt at verse's forge to shape a form both new and strange!" That would be the bewailing of a puzzled critic. Might be, then, one has yet to play a great deal with what has come and tease more truth and beauty from the reluctant giver of beauty and truth, that it becomes felicitously chaste and comprehendible. Might very well be that something is trying to come through, that it is still groping, and having not yet found itself is standing helplessly away from us. Might be it needs more time, more latitude, more love and fondling. Might be in a bespelled mood we have our own quick little ideas and there is the easy self-acclaim—"Arrah, sweet myself!"

But the voice of the unknown, though really not so feeble, is never harshly assertive and hence we should necessarily try to listen to it. Perhaps behind the puzzlement there is also the resolution of our difficulty when in the serene and composed mood of identification we perceive associations that are deeper and subtler and significantly meaningful. To understand and appreciate a suggestive language needs another type of sensitivity and acquiring that can be quite worthwhile, even spiritually rewarding.

Therefore, instead of worrying about the snippety makeup of the cantos presented here, we can view them in another manner, in the manner of an enviable bonsai. But can this cherished bonsai-image be applied to our cantos if in despair it is going to feel awfully dwarfed in the presence of the majestic Tree, if it is going to pant for breath in the atmosphere of light and delight? There could be a disparaging voice reproachful of it too. "Sorry, I don't like this bonsai," someone possibly will make a gruffish remark on seeing *Savitri* reduced to tiny play-toys called cantos. This criticism could be severe yet when taken along with Raymond Franck Piper's observation about *Savitri*: "We know that we must resort to the art of poetry for expressing, to the fullest possible artistic limits, the yearnings and battles of mankind for eternal life. Sri Aurobindo created what is probably the greatest epic in the English language and the longest poem in any language of the modern world. I venture the judgement that it is the most comprehensive, integrated, beautiful and perfect cosmic poem ever composed. It ranges symbolically from a primordial cosmic void, through earth's darkness and struggles, to the highest realms of supramental spiritual existence, and illumines every important concern of man, through verse of unparalleled massiveness, magnificence, and metaphysical brilliance."

Where would then in such massiveness and magnificence and

metaphysical brilliance this miniature bonsai handiwork park itself off? Perhaps nowhere. Spiritual poetry and *Savitri* in particular belong to another world and the best is to live in that realm of marvellous reality alone. But *Savitri* is also the happy encourager of creativity. Its electric charge can light orange-gold flames to brighten our lives. Living in it is also expressing in it. It gives us the truth to grow more and more in the dynamics of that truth. It never stifles an ardent soul's longings towards positive and fulfilling enjoyment of the spirit's beatitudes with their precious evocative presents. On the other hand, it has the power to bring closer to these longings and urges many splendours of love and beauty and truth's widenesses.

There is therefore a pretty reasonable hope for the bonsai also. The Japanese surely know for centuries the big joy of growing bonsai. For them cultivating bonsai is a very artistic hobby and there is nothing artificial in it. It can become for them an articulation of the sense of what is charming and attractive. To grow trees and plants in containers, that they look their most beautiful, is to live with nature in another warm and caring mood of inner concord. In it there is a high degree of aristocracy; there is even a measure of worshipful devotion to the Nature-Goddess of Beauty. There is almost a kind of spiritual relationship achieved through aesthetic Yoga. Through this new friendship with the majestic Tree an artist allows that majestic Tree to express freely in another way its dharmic characteristics, its individuality, all done without driving it to fit any particular category, and to help it achieve its most beautiful, its natural attractive balanced form. "Sometimes he will bend branches with wires or cut them off altogether. The key is never to force his will on it but to appreciate the dignity of each living plant and treat it with love and respect." And the nice thing about this bonsai art is that there is no such thing as a "finished" bonsai!

Bonsai is never a reduced photocopy of the original, just a concise representation in the carefully worked-out style of miniaturization in sculpture. It does not stem the essential features or provide a substitute for the true. In fact bonsai in the language of poetry possesses a possibility of creative selection leading to fresher interpretations. In the process when we go through choices there could enter exaggerations or distortions or aspects having their bearing on personal affect. None of these will constitute a lack of faithfulness, particularly when the spirit's liberties are assured in this creative enterprise. On the contrary, all this becomes a part of the day's happening and there is a joy in it, a joy that can also be richly meaningful and widening. At times it can even bring the radiance of an early hour or else a sudden revelation that can light up our obscurities. In the dark night of the soul where it is always three o'clock in the morning, there can break the subtler crimson or orange and brighten the sky with its mysterious glow. Perhaps it is that which will be most welcome in this language of poetry.

If we have to carry this bonsai-image farther, it could very much be said that each bonsai is a brief creation of an individual artist. The bonsai of a particular tree by different artists will be different, each carrying in it the aesthetic truth of its soul's reality as experienced by him in the deep meditative association with it. He might as well say that it is his bonsai. Its imaginative language can thus become intensely contemplative as well as personal. Each bonsai then turns into an opener of prospects which lie beyond our immediate sight. The truth that is not relative or pragmatic can step into the silence of our mind and mould our thoughts in its verities, can give pleasing and well-formed shapes to our life's questing moods. While understandably we might be somewhat skeptical about our capacity to find this truth, the chances are that an element of its expressive reality itself could yet enter in us. The *Savitri*-meditations will then have served the initial purpose of taking us in that truth's ambiance. These can themselves then become gateways leading us into her sun-worlds where breathe the dynamic expressive truths.

The Birth of Savitri

Canto One

At the river's bend hope took a northward turn—
As if stumbling on a strange post of the night
Stars found a sudden way through emptiness;
Something glimmered to awaken a newer urge,
The spirit of things timeless and alone.
Gods were yet to be and the enormous hush
Held in its still incumbent mood of trance
Another surprise getting shaped by death.
Colours of wonder flew on rhythmic wings,—
And also came repeated pain in the heart.
But in rich green silence of the wood at noon
Stood Savitri to meet the blemished might.

9 April 2002

Canto Two

Music streamed down from blue of the upper sky
And the hills and the lush fields and the choir birds
Bore its eager delight in earthly moments.
In emerald peace of that wilderness
Love came seeking her through hesitant ages:
A phoenix of flame-hued wings descending
Into death awaited her fiery greatness.
A joy of beauty bejewelled all her being
And her soul was a deep celebration
Of divinity in the strides of time;
Even her body recalled its godly longing.
This mortal world claimed its truth in her birth.

12 April 2002

Canto Three

A king-yogi willed her rush in the earthly fields,
Bright waters of her divinising force.
From a homeland of the truth, the right, the vast
Down the gold-white rays descended the sun;
It quickened a splendid fire on the altar
Of fate, the elemental ignorance.
An ancient sacrifice released his soul
And in a swift lunge tearing nature's bond
Sped abroad horses of spirit's energies.
A vision grew wider than the universe
And the unknowable's script became distinct.
Aloof he climbed heaven's ascending slopes.

14 April 2002

Canto Four

Concealed the spirit's immensities lie
And nature is all, nursing the age-old grief.
On life's tree time has built her nest of pain
And as the eternal's guard there stands death.
But her vision and work aim at heaven-fire
A-kindled in this half-lit terrestrial day.
An invisible presence prompts her movements
Even as in the mute trance of matter
Through dimness of her eyes looks out the sun.
Slowly the discoverer voyages on seas
Reaching calm waters across the cosmic shores
Where under the horned moon is adrift his barge.

19 April 2002

Nest of Pain: Keats

Canto Five

In the murky cave awoke the god of sleep
Who builds in trance the starry worlds of dream,
And Aswapati understood their meaning
And the spiritual sense in material things,
Grasped the will that works behind halting fate.
A Ganges of knowledge poured down from above
Flooding his mortality with supernal light.
In the listening depth of his heart he heard
Sounds that lead movements of the heavenly spheres,
Voices that disclose the cosmic secrecies.
He entered into wide excellent realms
And lived in the day of the undying spirit.

21 April 2002

Canto Six

Fourteen sounds came from Shiva's rattle-drum,
Fourteen waves surged on the ocean of calm;
Fourteen desires gathered in the world's desire.
From materials of these many worlds
Was formed this earth, darling of the dancer.
Angels, demons, gods of the great spirit
Took their stations up the viewless ladder
And poured their bounties on this little soul.
But haunted was she by a grisly shade
And Aswapati to redeem her woe
Sought a power beyond the afflicter's reach.
The seer within set him on the upward route.

23 April 2002

Canto Seven

First he entered the world of exquisite matter
That could beauty house and all its sweetness
And bring unflawed wonder to time-made things.
A quiet flame burned in the gold lamp of joy
And filled room and room with the light of its truth.
But then came mind and fragmented the dream;
A wave dashed on the hoary rock of night
And in its spume and spray dimly glistened
A million planktons of the vague early form,
And only lingered a fading memory.
Of yore there lived the atomic being alone,
Preparing the body of a deathless god.

25 April 2002

Canto Eight

Heavenly queen wore flowing purple dresses
In the sky and drove her car of adventure
On roads of swift brightsome mood. Sun nor moon
Nor countless stars of the unbounded world
Drew limits to life's zestful vineyard song.
Eagle-winged flying over the viewless Everest
Or a worm crawling on the Pacific's floor,
Is her spirit hazardously valiant.
No wonder, in her amaranthine craze
She hailed death and took him for her husband.
Out of that wedlock were born grim children,
But Aswapati discerned there another will.

28 April 2002

Canto Nine

Earth's thick shadow swallowed the bold angel
And in that occult mystery began
The quizzical march; the eclipsed moon of joy
Explored the emptiness with its blind regard,
Compelling yet the desert of the universe
To feel and flower in the laughter of god.
Soon out of dull matter's crevices hissed
Someone and from its terrifying fangs
Poured quick poison on the Cleopatran breast.
Yet she adventured into the Jurassic
And gave early thought to the Neanderthal.
A sense that suffered triple gloom was now here.

28 April 2002

Canto Ten

Crossing the destinies of sorrows and of joys
Child of jagat-shakti, the maimed goddess
Bore children in whom burned no gracious flame.
Soulless creatures lived feeding on slush
Or relished frog-liver cooked in cruelty
And, croaking throughout the night, hungered for more.
At times 'neath the life-mind squirmed a trepid ray
And looked at things with squinting scarlet eyes;
At times some ghost of thought rushed quickly by
Or the animal leaped to seize on wisdom's word.
Yet from elsewhere awareness must come
And bring gain to the godheads of little life.

30 April 2002

Jagat-Shakti: World-Force

Canto Eleven

Led by his spirit's promptings Aswapati
Reached the rainbow land where in colourful haste
The celestial artist created wonders.
Life sang golden reality's nether song
And a miracle was wrought in matter's womb.
Thus alone would it suffer the pregnant change,
The rock-image of Shiva beget offspring.
But presently all saw just a faint gleam
In the brute stuff wherein lies imprisoned
The idea that gives meaning to our lives,
As if failed the intention which bore truth.
A power that denied grace held her in sway.

2 May 2002

Canto Twelve

Another reality the spirit met.
A dark river flowed 'neath the currents of time
And swam gargantuan fish swallowing
Gargantuan fish, god's shadow only god.
On its grimy bank a citadel was built
And a fierce scarecrow shouted through the night.
In it stayed the fatal woman wearing
As a forehead mark destiny's black sun.
From the dreadfulness of her nixie past
Peered eyes that deepened the mystery of hell
Even as she proclaimed the Tao of evil.
But in that cave too Aswapati saw Vishnu.

4 May 2002

Canto Thirteen

In dismal river was born the tadpole ego
Who claimed forthwith the universe for its use
And brought falsehood to run the enterprise,
And hired a serpent to guard the sleeping treasure.
Soon in countless numbers burned these dark stars
Working out in the ways of night the fate
Ruinous of this creation, soul's quick downfall.
The terrible adventuress grew hostile
And gave to the interminable nothing
A chance to win divinity,—through death.
Then in the rocky insensate trance was heard
Wing-flap of birds and chime of distant bells.

5 May 2002

Canto Fourteen

If darkness gave to her a grimacing face,
Under the flowering acacia life was sweet,
A bloom of happiness in god's smiling grove.
Music trailed in the cadence of the stream
And the note of love gave wings to the singing bird,
King and queen strolled in the moonlit garden,
As if by a magic wand came a new world
Into birth to heal the wounds of the past.
A warm air urged the traveller on his way,
The chariot wheels setting into motion
Swift rhythms that trace the orbits for the suns.
In its rush a fiery wonder filled his soul.

5 May 2002

Canto Fifteen

Could it be that a great thought made the world,
Light plunged in the night and became fortunate stars
And life awoke feelings in the dumb mass
And the blue-tinged brain found its reason to be?
A thinking ape was not an accident
And the braying mind was not without design
And never was the atom elemental.
Yet was implanted denial in the dna
And a swift-footed pride in the forest raged
And a serene mistress read nature's tomes.
Still from the invisible fount of wisdom
Poured sudden truths that bring vision to our sight.

7 May 2002

Canto Sixteen

Ascending the slopes of mind Aswapati
Now stepped into a world of sapphire thought
That looks at unborn luminous ideas
Knowing themselves which live in spirit alone.
Needless here were reason's heavy glasses
And broadened the vista unto the unseen.
Magic word was a key for truth's locked cave
And numbers and forms became visible links
And doors of awareness led to Platonic gold.
So could he walk in eminence of these realms
And bright immortalities freely breathe.
Yet truth like sun is vaster than all its flames.

8 May 2002

Canto Seventeen

Mountains of time climbed towards timeless peaks
And god's felicities flamed high in god.
It was a silent chant, a pilgrim march
Of the petite who saw marvellous worlds
And soared in the calm of creation's joy.
The aspiring soul of earth breathed wonders
And the truth that answers made it beauteous.
In splendid will of the spirit was lit
A fire that gives to mortals seerhood
And raises the sacrifice to heaven.
A leader has arrived, friendly knower,
And he shall escort us on the shining path.

9 May 2002

Canto Eighteen

What of victory drums, what of the grieving heart?
Armies of Hitler set the world on fire,
Maniacs of time destroy the towers of pride,
And what of the river-song through luxuriant fields,
Of Sistine Chapel and the caves of Ajanta?
Aloof and untouched watches the witness eye,
Else consents to the whims in nature's play.
Passive has become the thinker, listless the thought,
And the Vedantist himself an illusion,
Gods, creatures, imperious death but shadows.
The will to be disappeared in that calm
And remained the mute alone and self-absorbed.

10 May 2002

Canto Nineteen

Shadows of night turned into splendours of god
And a delicate fragrance filled the air
And in the etheric hush surged forth sounds
That speak of the truer infinity's urgings;
The calm pace of the yogin-traveller
Took him to the temple-palace of Sophia,
Self-luminous and divine, creation's heart.
His will burned in the will of the bright goddess,
The builder of the worlds to build a new world.
Her almighty power he must house in his soul's deep —
Not for himself but to change the lot of man,
Bring immortal happiness to this deathful life.

11 May 2002

The World-Soul:
    Gnostic Sophia
    Goddess of Wisdom
    Apocalyptic Virgin
    Theotakos—Mother of God
    The Divine Feminine
    Swayamprabhā of the Ramayana

Canto Twenty

Then Brahma engaged himself in gold-bright tapas
And the directions were born and the word
And out of the truth-idea, the splendid womb
Sprang readily seven rhythms of creation
And the great rishis took radiant daughters
For their spouses and in their rich company
Held sessions of the undying triple fire,
Made offerings of the earth, the mid-region
And, when had set the sun, the blazing heaven.
And Aswapati partook in the hearth
And the table of the gods. His body-mind
Opened to things that are to come to time.

12 May 2002

Tapas: Intense spiritual concentration; the Yoga of the Will.
Triple Fire:
Householder's Fire, *grāhapatya*, morning offering, earth;
Ancestor's Fire, *dakṣhiṇa*, midday offering, mid-world or *antarikṣha*;
Fire of the Gods, *āhavanīya*, evening offering, heaven.
Sun-Lightning-Agni.
Hearth and Table of the Gods:
At the top of the human scale are the prophets, the minstrels and the
physicians; their next step upward is to the divine, sharing the hearth
and the table of the gods.—Empedocles.

Body-Mind: *tanū-manas.*

Canto Twenty-One

Into luminous emptiness he entered
And even the world's yearning which he carried
In his high-intended Odyssey disappeared.
A potent universe without galaxies,
Without streams, mountains, beasts or birds or men
Withheld in its formlessness the epiphanic.
Behind sachchidānanda was the quiescent
And what remained was nirvana of the absolute,
The austere apocalyptic alone.
Yet must be known that power whose enigma
Gives meaning and content to things of the world.
His spirit's will pursued the unknowable.

13 May 2002

Sachchidānanda: Truth-Consciousness-Bliss

Canto Twenty-Two

Then was abolished the eternal nay
And only the forceful positive stood there,
The fire that gives fire to a million fires.
Immortal death worked with the heart of love
And ignorance was a bright page in the book
Om Chidrūpinī Paramā, her name.
Sons of divinity hymned her glories
And offered to her onyxes and diamonds
And epic conquests of nobility
And real-ideas of distinction,
Found in her the secret of the Veda.
The incarnate soul was fulfilled in her.

14 May 2002

Om Chidrūpiṇī Paramā:
Om, she whose form is consciousness, supreme.

Canto Twenty-Three

But the heavy past weighing on the soul of the earth
He must offer to the flames of sacrifice,
Of nature and gods, kindled in the new divine.
Here was the beginningless beginning
And the endless end, here the unmoved mover.
Here flamed his will in trance of luminous sleep
And was formed the world celebrating truth
Immortal even in things material.
Thus broke out the yoga's paean supreme.
The stork of paradise brought the news of a birth
Waiting for voiceless omniscience to speak.
Opened were freeways for haste of the daughter.

15 May 2002

Canto Twenty-Four

Even as Aswapati invoked Savitri
With many-leaping flames in the radiant sky
Rained over his tapas resplendent waters.
The dreams of earth excelled in their rapid flow
And the auspicious hour validated the world.
True, the gods enter not this den of night
And the dark-hued sphinx slays the soul of man
And time is haunted by the ghost of death;
But if life is to discover love's immensity
And sunbright children are to be born in these bounds,
She must take our mortal birth and alter fate.
The word was spoken and the new era began.

16 May 2002

Savitri:
In the story by Vyasa as we have in the Mahabharata, the issueless
king Aswapati offers daily a hundred-thousand oblations to Goddess
Savitri. He performs the Yajna for eighteen years.

Canto Twenty-Five

Year is the body and Savitri was born.
Gods and goddesses gave her heavenly gifts,
The moon of delight, the sword of triumph,
The golden heart of love, the mind of light,
The physical plastic to the touch of truth,
The spirit making the moulds of time immortal.
Even as a child she would visit the stars
Or dream of a city waking to wide days.
Already the earth's longings took bright wings,
Already the ancient promises became good,
Already the faultless charm drew closer the worlds.
Her presence attracted great divinities.

17 May 2002

Canto Twenty-Six

The young princess grew phase by phase, the moon,
And the roundsome digit gladdened beauty's sky.
In her dreamful slumber and in her bright waking
The wheels of time speeded on a jewelled path
And life became a journey led by love.
She could hold in her happy embrace the whole world
And pour the wine of rapture in human heart;
But the frail vessel shudders with its joy.
High the eagle of her flaming youth ever flew,
Above wind and cloud unmatched and alone.
No earth-soul could reach her splendour's winging,
No Aryan prince claim her hand in marriage.

17 May 2002

Canto Twenty-Seven

In the royalty of hush sometimes descends
The word that can forever change destiny
And bring good even to death's circumstance:
Eternity's moment arrives on white wings
And a cry is stirred in quiet of the soul;
Something surges from the creation's silence
And to flute-call awakes the beloved's heart.
From the world of immortality she had come
Not to fly a lonely flight in heavens
Of joy but into life's rough countries to dare.
Far in the forest on an emerald bough
Awaits the gold-bright orange-hued doomed bird.

18 May 2002

Canto Twenty-Eight

Her future's course ran through the karmic past
And the chariot-wheels recalled the dim tracks
Of memory as if to claim godheads
Who drive the speeds of nature across birth
And birth when silent watches the alert eye.
No human escort led the events of time,
But love seated in the heart of Savitri
Spurred the toiling energies towards their goal.
She heard the sounds of the Veda chanted
In the ear and sight opened the soul's doors
And infinity's calm reposed in her bosom.
Golden solitude stood waiting for the hour.

19 May 2002

Canto Twenty-Nine

Mango-blossoms burst in the yellow's richness
And the air was filled with delicate fragrance
And the distant coïl sang a welcome song.
Far were left behind the kings' palaces
And the rivers threading proud cities of time
And the gods dwelling in luminous shrines
And meditation's groves awake to the spirit.
She now reached a place where absent was life's buzz
And mind needed not the tracks of thought to run.
There close to Shiva's fane came seeking her
The flame of love in a body of death
And blazed in a sudden moment the idol.

19 May 2002

Canto Thirty

Through the Shalwa tapovanas as she moved
In the lotus of her heart opened a pink sun,
Splendid in the summer of eternity.
Though born in transient world his tranquil gaze
Was a look of the spirit winning nature's joys
And his dawns were the gifts of her wisdom.
The one whom she met in the sudden forest
Gave bright deservance to the dreams of her life—
Even as he discovered the charmed moon
Of beauty in the chariot of his delight.
Gods and goddesses gathered in the sky
And calm was heard the chiming of happy bells.

20 May 2002

*tapovana*s: the forests where the ancient rishis were engaged in
tapas, the spiritual austerities and sacrifices.
Chariot of Delight: *chandraratha* of the Rig Veda.

Canto Thirty-One

God's Savitri and goddess's Satyavan
Courted the green fields of life together.
If love urged her divinity to step out
And spread beauty's spell over his mortal soul,
The beloved brought a skyful of sweetness
And healed his wounds, of cleaved matter and spirit.
Beings of glad worlds thronged the forest grove
And flocks of birds came from the hilltops
And dimpling waters ran with murmuring notes
And wild flowers scattered their joy in the air
And doe and buck pranced in blithesome grass
And priests of nature chanted the marriage hymn.

21 May 2002

Canto Thirty-Two

But a black tiger stood on the stealthy way
And Narad saw him from his home in Vaikuṇṭha
And hastened that be known to Savitri
Year is the body and Satyavan,
When fly away twelve birds of time, shall die.
In the earthly soil was cast the occult seed,
An imponderable wonderful, bright.
No human mind would comprehend its working,
No heart's passion halt the advancing doom,
And truer yet became Savitri's resolve.
If love came from the old creation to die
The new shall take birth in the glory of death.

21 May 2002

Vaikuṇṭha: The Heaven of Vishnu

Canto Thirty-Three

Falsehood is the sorrow of the supreme
And not for nothing was this creation made
And not for failure the sacrifice performed.
Not this world but pain is deep illusion
And when the price is paid it turns into joy.
But only the great in soul can bear its stroke
And walk through death as through door of the sun.
Savitri must wage the battle for god
And meet the stark force in the flame of her will.
Her way to the high runs through the bosom of night
And when is kindled the fire in trance of sleep
She can house victory's power and the challenge face.

22 May 2002

It is as though the battle of the world was being fought within my
consciousness. (The Mother, *Notes on the Way*, 25 October 1972,
CWM, Vol. 11, p. 323)

Canto Thirty-Four

The shadow of bliss now fell on Savitri.
In the trance of awesome night when together
Her moon of honey was chased by a poison cloud
And the owl of fear hooted in the sobbing heart
And reached to console her voice of no helpful god.
Not forbidding dream but unspeaking silence
Appeared to make the year harsher than grief.
The flame that had come with her from the calm sky
Trembled in the storm-wind raging in the forest
And instantly marked destiny drew nearer yet.
In the embrace of Satyavan and Savitri
Laughed death deriding this life's hollowness.

23 May 2002

Canto Thirty-Five

Savitri lay prone with sorrowing spirit,
But the greatness who watches all her movements
Commanded her to awake to her soul's truth
And gather in it the defeatless power
And, crossing the gate of death, meet the eternal.
First in subconscient plunge the shadowy past
Unfolded to her sight the obscure worlds,
The wounding stone, the hungry beast, the ape-mind
Leaping from tree to dangerous tree of thought.
Somewhere lived deep buried the issue of nature
Finding in subterranean dark its food.
This she must consume in her shakti yajna.

24 May 2002

Shakti Yajna: The sacrifice performed to get power.

Canto Thirty-Six

From the body's guarded fort Savitri stepped
Into a bleak room that housed ghastly beings,
Pythonesses and she-wolves ever waiting
To tear the soul of man, kill it with untruth,
Night-ravens crying on the path to perdition.
But she braved the assault and breathed freer air.
Past the dim chapels, past the garden schools,
The viharas of monks, the adwaitins' maṭhas,
She met en route to the cave where dwells the flame
Brilliant gods helping with their light our lives,
Bringing to wakened sense things of the spirit.
But she yearned for the birth of the child divine.

25 May 2002

*vihāra*s and *maṭha*s are lonely cloisters of the respective ascetics.

Canto Thirty-Seven

Now the little boroughs of dream were left behind
And she came to a place where toil consorts
Of the triple purusha, suffer to change
Nature that body and life and mind's self
Open to the supraliminal powers.
Portions of the secret soul of Savitri,
Unwearied, and conquering, and tranquil-bright,
They bring profounder gods to struggling earth.
But what if the antagonists raise their heads,
Or take up arms against the descending sea!
She must discover in the fullness of night
A flame that can hold deathless might in its blaze.

26 May 2002

Triple Purusha: instinctive, impulsive and emotional-intellectual being
presiding over the actions of the three nature-powers: compassionate
toiler and warrior on the battlefield and luminous in wisdom, full of
Karuna, Jnana-Prem-Ananda, Prakash-Harsha-Shanti.

Canto Thirty-Eight

Now the way must cut through brahmāndhāra
And Savitri meet god in a godless form.
By whatever it may be known or perceived
That ceases in the genuine night, the sacred void,
And only remains the will that cancels
The burden of death present in the mortal's breast.
Above all stood the wonder of the triple sun,
Bliss and consciousness and absolute truth.
Suddenly the cave opened and she saw
The primal force seated on the topaz rock
And heard seven great notes; flooded her the sound
Occult soham-om-ham-yam-ram-vam-lam.

26 May 2002

Brahmāndhāra: Darkness of Brahma or the Great Night, the Night of God; Dryden's is genuine night full of idiocy and ignorance.

soham, om, ham, yam, ram, vam, lam are the seven sounds that come from the seven Chakras, from above below, in the subtle-physical. The seven musical notes *sā, re, ga, ma, pa, dha, nī* or *do, re, mi, fa, sol, la, si* have their origin in these centres rising from below above.

Canto Thirty-Nine

The lamp of her soul burned in a fruitful darkness
Where quiet void became a means to dissolve
The inherent issue of first mortality
Carrying yet in its backward-moving will
The mystery of this creation's godlessness.
So her luggage of time she left behind
To bring to it the treasures of the true,
To thought plenitudes of the silent spirit.
All now vanished in that nirvanic calm
And in the siddhi of nature's dissolution
She joined back with the origin, love alone.
Then the form behind the impersonal grew bright.

27 May 2002

siddhi: a settled spiritual realisation
She joined back with the Origin:
    The Mother's experience of 1 October 1958
    Agenda, Vol. 1, pp. 198, 202-03.

Canto Forty

But perhaps she would have slipped into that peace,
Forgetting the world, forgetting her Satyavan.
To the danger awoke the spirit of the earth
And it took awhile for Savitri to be.
Now light in the water and the smooth pebbles
Glistening with the sense of fairer life breathed joy
And the rishis of the forest suddenly felt
A new divinity invading them,
And stood creation's reality distinct.
A chant of the name filled her body's cells
And in it joined countless aspiring voices.
In matter's heart was blown the conch of triumph.

28 May 2002

Canto Forty-One

The sky was crowded with a throng of gods
And golden Durga with sword in her hand
Guarded the kingly tree since the early dawn
And Satyavan and Savitri moved in the peace
Of that rich forest, destiny's rendezvous.
Year is the body and Satyavan must die
And three great times he uttered the mantric name.
The noon was filled with the creator's shadow
And the still river watched the motionless crane,
As if eternity had come to its end.
In the campanile of death tolled the hour
And no more was there Savitri's Satyavan.

30 May 2002

Canto Forty-Two

The luminous flame left the clay-lamp behind
And, impelled by the path, walked into the night.
Now the old man with his chill pitiless look
Determined the movement of the captive poor,
Helpless mortality yielding to the fear
Terrible, the keeper of the souls of the dead.
But someone assumed charge of human Savitri
And she gathered within the strength that puts out death
And took courage to follow the god to the end.
In the oceanic surge of her silent will
Rested the exultant power that can save
The world from the fate of collapsing time.

31 May 2002

Canto Forty-Three

Enraged by her firm intruding tread the person
Of the abyss swung back, as though agonised
The night grew more dreadful in her terror.
Nothing seemed meaningless and a graver aim
Sustained its might against the spirit's assault.
Imperious the voice bade her to return—
With boons in his bosom the deceased held dear.
But Savitri steadfast in the truth of her soul
Was alert to the reality of the world.
What boons these if earth remains ever death-bound!
From flames of the pyre must rise the birds of joy
And awakened dawns bring to life their love.

1 June 2002

Canto Forty-Four

If death were not there life would disappear,
Even as would sweetness when absent is spite.
The abiding ender of the worlds must work
And uphold the marvellous claim of the soul,
Or else our superficial mortality
Never would suffer change and the dream-ideal
Find not a place to live in god's vastnesses.
Hence Satyavan through countless martyrdoms
Must advance and do well on the occult way.
But like a volcano burning upside down
A will lived in the mystery of the night
And saw the charming that can be true on earth.

2 June 2002

Canto Forty-Five

Things of beauty were there in death's dream world
And all around prince Satyavan cast a spell
Of joy and honeyed life breathed fragrant truths.
But hope flounders on the rock of darkness
And a helpless phantom screams in the cloud
And incarnate gods depart in agony
And vain is the yearning to change this doleful earth,
An illusion to see love in the mortal's breast.
What mind if the horses of passion it reins not,
And what soul if it blooms not on the tree of time?
But Savitri let stream from her heart music,
Not dream but a roaring fire of happiness.

2 June 2002

Canto Forty-Six

Is it not ananda that flows in a stream?
And ananda that surges in the calm ocean,
A wave of ananda on the waters of ananda,
And the boat of ananda and the winds of ananda,
The nest of ananda on the tree of ananda,
Ananda of death and ananda in death,
At the base, in the middle, on the summit
Ananda, ananda, all ananda!
O death to fill great life with ananda!
But victory in life wins not great death
And a nobler sacrifice must be kindled
And the supreme with his flaming spouse preside.

3 June 2002

Ananda: The highest creative Bliss founded on Reality.

The Mother speaks of life only without death as a blind attempt:
Agenda, Vol. 6, pp. 235-37.

Canto Forty-Seven

But existential death armed with law
Respects not cloying lyricism of delight
And scoffs at wisdom that is not held by strength.
Golden paradise on earth is a dream
Paradisal and Savitri is naïve
That nature and spirit would consort here,
As if the truth-gods harboured an illusion
That the great sun would burn in body's house.
Adamant the dreadful will of darkness stood,
Dismissing hope of the mortal's return to life.
But the flaming woman on battleground
Took charge of god's work and fled the denial.

4 June 2002

Canto Forty-Eight

The embodied nihil fled—only to appear
As the tempter divine behind the void,
The new gate through which Savitri forced the way
To claim Satyavan in the world of her choice,
The world of men and matter and joyous things.
Far behind were left the original creations
And in the tremendous hour of reality
She made her will one with the supreme's will
And in the luminous hush of her heart
Exultant rose truth-word of the topaz sky.
Then hurried the glad hymn of sweetness and love
And resplendent awoke the soul of earth to the sun.

5 June 2002

Canto Forty-Nine

Happy life rushed in bird and beast and tree
And through dreaming quietude ran swift joys of men
And the rishis in the forest felt a change,
As though the past had vanished into fire
Of the yajna kindled to make wide the world.
Satyavan and Savitri tended the flames,
Flames whose tongues can bear expression of the true,
Hold in their leaping zest newborn greatnesses.
Moon-lotuses bloomed for the crimson bright
And Soma and Indra and Agni and Vayu
Came in their auspicious forms to celebrate
The birth of Savitṛ in this creation.

5 June 2002

savitṛ: The Sun-God.

Sri Aurobindo's Gayatri:

> *tat savitur varam rūpam jyotiḥ parasya dhīmahi*
> *yannaḥ satyena dīpayet.*

> Let us meditate on the most auspicious form of Savitri,
> the Light of the Supreme
> which shall illumine us with the Truth.

Résumé of *Savitri*

I: 1 The Symbol Dawn

Savitri begins with the primordial Darkness when the gods are still asleep. Out of it has to come a fuller divine manifestation upon earth. But obstructing its path there is the mind of ominous Night and nothing can happen as long it is present. Many were the attempts made earlier but the success was only partial. At times something had stirred on the borderline of dream and waking, but too feeble was the awareness. Again and again the dawn had come with her gifts and had to go back as there was no sufficient response. It is in this circumstance that Savitri, the Daughter of the Sun-God, takes human birth. She identifies herself with this death-bound earthly creation with all its suffering. Keeping her spirit open to the Spirit in all she takes up the issue. To make the anguished body a receptacle of heavenly joy has been her ancient mission. She recalls it and yogically prepares herself to confront the Adversary. This shall be on the day of Satyavan's death.

I: 2 The Issue

Satyavan awaits in the forest of life the arrival of Savitri. His waiting for her is, in the cosmic working, the waiting of the God of Love for her. For him she is perfection's home and could well live in her as in his own infinity. But behind him also follows covertly the God of Death. Savitri is yet unaware of it. But while she is reviewing the past a supernatural darkness surrounds her. In it her will rises to cancel that past itself. Hers is a struggle in which neither the Gods of the Sky nor the Powers of Nature can lend any help to her. But at the opportune hour the Goddess in her stands out revealed and at once takes charge of things and events. Savitri as a defeatless warrior falls upon Death and the bounds of Consciousness and Time break open. All this has already happened in the transcendental realm, but now it must be worked out on earth.

I: 3 The Yoga of the King: The Yoga of the Soul's Release

The divine Goddess takes mortal birth. She is in a way compelled to do so. She comes as Savitri in answer to Aswapati's prayer. In the context of the creation's issue he carries with him the world's desire and invokes her to incarnate. For that he engages himself in the triple Yoga, the Individual, the Universal, and the Transcendental Yoga. This Yoga is done in earth-consciousness to prepare the needed base for her birth and action. Aswapati himself as the Supreme incarnate accepts the burden. First he releases himself from Nature's hold. He finds the source from which his spirit came, knows his larger self and becomes one with all. But there is the ingrained reluctance in the earthly stuff. He must discover its cause and remove it. He does it. Now his body's parts also open to higher things, to greater light. With the soul's release Aswapati has achieved everything as an individual. There must now come the spirit's freedom from all contingencies.

I: 4 The Secret Knowledge

But perhaps there is a purpose in the Spirit submitting itself to Nature's law, Being to the law of Becoming, Purusha obeying Prakriti. It is through her mechanics that this stubborn inconscient stuff can slowly gain awareness. Though not herself divine presently, she is planned divinely. This truth has to be found and the intention yogically worked out. Aswapati is therefore engaged in the Yoga of Knowledge of the Time-Born Man. He now gets a new vision of himself and of the world. He may not be yet aware of the goal fixed for him, not know whether he is going to reach just the featureless unseen or discover a new mind and body in the city of God. But he is tied to the fate of this creation and there cannot be rest for him until the dusk from man's soul is lifted. He must attend to it.

I: 5 The Yoga of the King: The Yoga of the Spirit's Freedom and Greatness

Aswapati first has the knowledge about the possibilities waiting for the time-born man. He has read the secret Vedic text and deciphered the significance of the great world rhythms. He sees a hidden sun even in the depth of darkness. His will now assumes superhuman dimensions and it can bring down a greater world. But he also discerns the gulf between what is and what is to be. He withdraws from everything and in silent mind hears the call. A Descent leaps down and there is a new change. Nothing now remains sealed to his sight. Where could abide only for a while the heavenlier states, there is no more resistance of the lower members. Nature is mastered and the exploration of her vast provinces begins. His present Raj Yoga, the Yoga of the King, has to be raised to the Cosmic Yoga, Vishva Yoga, and finally to the Yoga of Surrender to the Divine Mother.

II: 1 The World-Stair

The Vishva Yoga begins. Here is a Universe well-planned and many-tiered. It has limits neither in Space nor in Time. Experience after experience displays the rainbow moods of the Power that brought it into existence. It is as if from one string issued out numberless harmonies, each with its own frozen perfection. They climb one above the other and disappear in the original Hush. It is up on these ascending slopes of Heaven that the aspiring soul of man moves. So too these worlds influence in several ways the working of this earth, her grief and her joy. Our souls were attracted by its mystery and accepted the travail. In the process slowly the meaning of the cosmic scheme itself becomes evident. The Seer is born within and whatever knowledge is necessary is received. In the exploration of this scheme no term has been fixed for Aswapati and his march is towards the indiscernible end. He sees Nature's climbing hierarchy and sets himself on the way.

II: 2 The Kingdom of Subtle Matter

The first port of entry is the world of Subtle Matter. Here are present the prototypal forms, the shining origins of things on earth. All here is beautiful, faultless, dream-hued, outlasting death and birth. Though so close to earth they suffer no deformation. Even as the soul is radiant, material substance in this region bears the signature of power and authority. From here occurs the fall into darker and denser reality that is ours. This makes us humble, but also can make us noble to be stars. Here is a possibility of our mortal body becoming glorious if it should hold sufficient truth in it. The divine substance is now present in this proximate world marking a new beginning towards that divinity on earth. But prior to that Aswapati has to discover what lies beyond this material Paradise.

II: 3 The Glory and Fall of Life

Not symmetric charm and carved dreams, but the spirit of adventure is what gives vibrancy to existence. Life bothers the least about the pros and cons and hazards to assert herself in every circumstance. Her high birth disdains not her entering into the squalid earth. Indeed, whatever can serve her questing delight she gambles on, unmindful of the peril. She risks even the extremes. Be they meadows of laughter or fields of toil, for her everything is for creative enjoyment. Because of her alone the dull material substance becomes sensitive to dynamic possibilities of the revealing Spirit. She builds the foundation for greater powers to step into this physical manifestation. However, in the process, Matter's stiffness or *jadatva* overpowers her and she is no more here her freer happier old self. Life meets Death and they together now drive the insecure cart of dubious immortality.

II: 4 The Kingdoms of the Little Life

The great power has succumbed and earth failed to keep the joy she had brought with her. Not only that. She herself has become an abject being crawling in the lowly mud. Yet in her arrival glimmers a faint hope urging the mortal's soul on the wakened path. Aswapati sees this pitiful state of fallen Life surviving on Death. Here perpetuity is her immortality. But then there are in this meaningful fall gains also. There is a climbing of life from below. The first creation is followed by the instinct of a thinking sense. An animal experiment then begins. In it all is done to satisfy the body's wants and survival of the fittest becomes the law. But with the physical mind opening to higher Light the possibility of transformation becomes distinct. Presently an instrument personality is born and all is dictated by habits. Everything looks species-based and repetitive; around the little glow of life there is the nescient haze.

II: 5 The Godheads of the Little Life

There is nothing that can be called angelic in this empire of little life. Chaos governs the infernal creatures inhabiting it. Life has force and she is driven by idea, but the Idea-Force is absent. Instinct is followed by thought and thought by will. Out of this queer stuff was shaped man and it could be proclaimed that he was well made. Still man lives just for a brief while—only to enjoy and suffer and die. He has essentially remained the same, yet greatly prone to error. His mind is but a puppet manipulated by unseen forces and such cannot be the end of Life's very desirable adventure. She has to move forward to receive truer gifts from the hands of Fortune. Not Man nor Nature but the Avatar alone can help her receive these rewards. He pays the price for that. If the body's cells have to be filled with divine joy he has to eliminate the wrong afflicting them. Sacrificing his triple glory he accepts the mortal state, bears its anguish. Aswapati moves through it with his spirit's alert flame.

II: 6 The Kingdoms and Godheads of the Greater Life

Stepping into the wider Life, Aswapati notices her attempt to seize the boundless in birth. Thus she would claim back her heavenly state she had lost long ago. She made this creation of many hues but missed the True. Yet she moves on towards the far-off Light. Aswapati glimpses a ray of hope in her thousand expressions. He hears the heartbeats of a hidden reality. But he also hears the weeping of her soul within. She has become hostile and has consorted herself with hidden death. She is a riddle unto herself and yet slays the puzzled wayfarer. But Aswapati reads clearly the hieratic script and the Word of Life is not a mystery to him. He discerns the gap between what she came to do and what she now is. Pause she would not in her attempt to bring glory to the material inanity, though her knowledge be incomplete. He must probe in the night itself for the cause of this failure.

II: 7 The Descent into Night

The problem of Life's abysmal condition is a central issue and Aswapati cannot rest content without tackling it. What could have been in the service of good has become an instrument of vice. In this world of fallen Life fair is foul and foul fair. If there is creative Darkness engendering pain, wickedness, suffering, corrupting truth, then it could be here. Now Ignorance, Falsehood, Error, Ego walk in its thick shadow and the Satanic votaries proclaim: "Evil, be thou my God." Life in that gloom with her perilous charm and beauty lies cursed under the Gorgon spell. There Aswapati felt that his body was licked by the hostile Power and he suffered fear. But this had to be borne. He endures and with his bare spirit masters her. The stepping of the Incarnate into the worlds of Night is a wonderful thing that can happen to her and in it is her opportunity to change.

II: 8 The World of Falsehood, the Mother of Evil and the Sons of Darkness

God created Hell in his mood of infinite love and justice, but this love has to first conquer the appalling Inane. The existential problem is the denial to all that is God's. Here are titans and maniac powers and cruel operators; here, allowed by the mighty Spirit, work determinedly terrible agencies. But Aswapati in the strength of his soul takes up the challenge. He probes penetratingly this kingdom of pain, this world of sorrow and hate, of wickedness and malignancy. Not only that. Shiva-like he drinks all the poison, till not a drop is left. The luminous truth in him yet remains intact. In the vastness of Existence he even feels the smallness of this queer material creation. Aswapati observes that the inconscient Being is asleep and knows not what it built. But he puts his finger upon the error and the pain and at once awakens there new knowledge. He has opened the Book of Bliss and Life's truth is revealed. The dichotomy between Matter and Spirit is resolved.

II: 9 The Paradise of the Life-Gods

In the occult abyss was the rendezvous with the Night. Aswapati had gone there to woo her dark and dangerous heart. On the track leading to the meeting place his footprints have become the seals of divinity and thence shall gush radiant fountains. Around him all is felicitous and wonderful and the daylight of conscious suns is within him. After that wounding experience here is something healing and marvellous. The dread is over and an Elysian fragrance fills the air. He is in the company of Gods and Goddesses and is thrilled with beauty, peace, love, might, desire, pleasure, dream, sweetness. Forms are shaped here by the divine light and mind is made immortal by music. Aswapati's whole being is flooded with bliss and an undying power fills his strength. But he has also the sure perception that this cannot be the journey's end and that the Highest must be reached.

II: 10 The Kingdoms and Godheads of the Little Mind

Across the land of sensuous beauty are the realms of observation and understanding. Now in the play of Nature has been set into motion another faculty, that of the early mind. First appears the physical mind, marking the beginning of the thinking mind. It is tied to habits and it toils in ignorance. Soon arrives Reason. She has come and made great inventions, built philosophies and rational disciplines, drawn on the map of knowledge a few lines of reality. But there is no goal and the game is inconclusive. In the process she stumbles upon the fissioned atom and in it sees the omnipotent's force. Yet what is witnessed is the tyranny of Matter's logic imposed upon the Spirit's swiftness of thought. There has to be a greater Mind to see a greater truth. Only rarely does intuition bring to us superior knowledge, the higher gnosis. Sometimes Life-Thoughts come like shining Maruts, or else the pure Thought-Mind brings bodiless ideas in our midst.

II: 11 The Kingdoms and Godheads of the Greater Mind

But these wonderful powers of Mind are not of great avail. There is a truth by which things can be seen in an unerring manner and that is altogether beyond their reach. Aswapati now meets in the Ideal's world the Thinker or Manishi. Across the first realms of Mind he is in the company of shining archangels and kings of thought. Theirs is an attempt to grasp Truth's absolute. The creative Word sets into motion these many worlds and the will-to-be is seized in things. The divine power of hearing comes as a natural gift. But Mind is incapable of understanding these works of Truth. Even sages and seers find her to be beyond their grasp. There is no way to know her and it is only by surrendering to the absolute will of hers that a ray of her radiant wonder can enter into our life's many dimnesses. Or else she would remain forever unknown to us.

II: 12 The Heavens of the Ideal

But the Ideal is always a bright spur for the explorer. At each step is seen a luminous world rising in honour of the high Truth. On one side are the kingdoms of love, beauty, joy, sweetness all bringing to earth their gracious marvels. What remained dormant until now opens to spiritual greatnesses. Here is felt the Immortal's touch. On the other side of this climbing pathway burns the deathless flame of will, the force of utter divine consciousness. Even as it climbs the ascending slopes, there is a call to reach the summits of existence. Aswapati moves through these worlds with the household ease. But he finds that here while beauty and greatness, sweetness and might, the Rose and the Flame, come together yet they stand apart. They would not find themselves in the single soul of the world. The spiritual path and the occult-psychic path run parallel but do not yet become one. Aswapati must therefore advance towards the diviner spheres.

II: 13 In the Self of Mind

On his onward march Aswapati has now entered the passive world of the superior being of Mind who is simultaneously impersonal also. He stands on the summit and is a silent witness, *sākshi*, of things carried out by Nature, Prakriti. He watches indifferently the good and the bad of life; he is unconcerned about victory or defeat. Yet without his consent the movements of Prakriti would not take place. He is *anumantā*, giving approval for her actions. Aswapati lived in this still self, and its quiet vastness was in him. But there was no urge to stay in it. That self seemed but a shadow of a vaster and more forceful a reality. Peace is all right, but there has also to be the Truth's dynamism. It is this dynamic aspect which gives credibility to this world. Aswapati found love and sweetness of the Mother-force absent here. This would not satisfy him and he is prompted to go beyond the realization of this silent self.

II: 14 The World-Soul

In search of the active power who shapes the course of events, Aswapati is led by a mysterious sound and he comes to a wonderful realm. There consciousness, mind, life, body are all made of soul-stuff and spiritual sense is the instrument of knowledge. Those who have by the practices of virtue accumulated great merit in life on earth ascend to this splendid abode. Here wait the liberated souls for a new adventure in the world of opportunities. Beyond it are regions of happiness and peace, of light, hope, love. Aswapati grows aware of them. He sees Shiva and Shakti in a fulfilling union's poise. Behind them stands the omnipotent Goddess, Chidvilasini or Consciousness-Force by whose act this creation has come out from the Unknowable.

Aswapati's spirit has now become a vessel to hold her luminous might. In her he finds an answer to his long search and surrenders to her. Indeed, this is the offering of the World-Soul to the Higher Power who alone can assure the success of his work. His quest bears fruit in her.

II: 15 The Kingdoms of the Greater Knowledge

Aswapati, after such a wonderful experience on the border touching the Transcendent, returns to the things of cosmic Time. Now wherever he goes he carries along with him the consciousness of Passive Brahman, the quiescent Sachchidananda as a foundation for all of his activities in the world. He sees the powers that supervise the world and beyond them looks for that which can bring about a universal change. He makes a total yogic surrender to the Reality which sustains the Earth, the Mid-region, and Heaven,—Bhur, Bhuvar, Swar. In that sacrifice he is newborn and even his body partakes in its joy. Yet this supernal birth is his alone and cannot be of great avail for the collective on the earth. The individual's supernal birth has to become a larger supernal birth. Its key is with the Divine Mother and therefore Aswapati must approach her. With this Siddhi attained, and with the cosmic forces now under his control, he becomes the Lord of Life, justifies his name Aswapati. Henceforth his march is towards that transcendence where is her home.

III: 1 The Pursuit of the Unknowable

The one whom Aswapati met standing behind the World-Soul is still a mystery to him. So his quest continues and he ascends to the height where stands only the bare Reality. But on that summit of realization he has to make a final choice,—he must either abandon the world and merge into that Reality or else seek that which will transform it. Towards that choice no help was available and the cosmic spirit remained just an aspect of Non-being, the first Asat. But that Asat is ever inaccessible. Perhaps in it if all should vanish then the golden Sphinx might reveal something of her mystery. But it entails a danger, that of going out of the manifestation. That eventuality would mean the failure of the soul's mission itself. Though to free the self from the contingent Nature is a basic condition for any progress, there is also an obligation of fulfilling oneself here.

Aswapati is alert to it and hence he must remove the veil of light.

III: 2 The Adoration of the Divine Mother

In that self-discovery Aswapati comes to know about God's desire that works here even in this mortal world. Here he is rewarded. It is in response to the longing of his soul that a being of wisdom, power, delight,—*jnāna, shakti, ānanda,*—steps out of eternity. He surrenders to her and his heart is glad. Existence no more seems to be without aim. In her is found the hidden Word, the Mantra of Ascent and Transformation. She stands at the head of this creation and she is the one who helps us cross great distances that yawn between us and the marvels that shine over there. From her Sun we can set alight our suns, suns of knowledge, strength, beauty, sweetness, love, joy, harmony, perfection. It is she who can turn our pain of death into ecstasy of life. How wonderful to be caught in her intolerant flame! Her light and her bliss he asked for men on earth. Nothing else he yearned for and gave himself entirely to her alone.

III: 3 The House of the Spirit and the New Creation

Aswapati sits expectantly with a prayer in his silent heart, but nothing happens. He is puzzled and must discover if something in him was still resisting the great advent. He is aware that even the least element could spoil the work. He traces its roots and extracts them out completely. He is free and enters into the superconscient state. There Nature's afflictions disappear and in the deep hush is the anticipation of an answering voice. Aswapati's solitary concern is the good of the grieving creature. His long tapasya was for that purpose. Indeed, it is out of it that sprang up a new creation in the transcendent. But it ought to become a part of the evolutionary reality. For that to happen the Spirit's disdainfulness towards Matter should disappear. Behind the present world Aswapati sees a world to be and the question is to make it actual. He knows that it can be done only by the divine Power. He must call her.

III: 4 The Vision and the Boon

There is a sudden flow of energy and Aswapati feels its rush into all parts of his being down to the very physical. Spirit and body identify with each other, even as the radiant Goddess stands in front of him. She counsels him not to force mortality's issue; he should instead leave all to the course of the evolving Time. He is told that Man is too weak to bear the burden of the Truth and he must graduate himself to receive her gifts. In the meanwhile, Aswapati should help this struggling creature on his heavenward march. She is ready to grant a boon to Aswapati, with the assurance that all things shall happen in God's transfiguring hour. But the Siddha Yogi makes himself bold and holds out an alternative. He knows that a new creation in the House of the Spirit is waiting to be born and the Goddess should incarnate herself to make it real here. Saying 'Be it so' the Goddess withdraws and glad Aswapati returns to attend to his worldly duties.

IV: 1 The Birth and Childhood of the Flame

The six tropical seasons have speeded through the year and the Goddess of eternal Time has stepped into earthly cycles. Savitri's arrival, marking a signal moment of the gods, is a beauty's festival in the bright and colourful Spring, the chosen season who brings joy to our mortal life. In it shall happen happier and wondrous things, unblemished by death. Indeed, in her birth have taken the heavenly charm and wonder a human body. She has accepted our transient lot, and its travail, in order to accomplish the divine task here. Savitri grows, becomes a student and a scout and a brave warrior. She is dear to everyone in every respect. In every act and thought and feeling of hers is expressed more and more of nobility of the high spirit. An invisible sunlight flows in her veins and her movements display the large significances of life. Her worship and prayer and aspiration become a call which draws an answer from absolute Destiny moulding our mortality.

IV: 2 The Growth of the Flame

Savitri's life opens doors for the secret powers to enter into gracious fields of activity. She acquires the lore of the world, learns its many philosophies and sciences and arts and crafts. But by her native right she also sees something beyond them. She is aware of the universal Self and in her embrace stay all, that she might breathe living happiness into them. But scarcely is recognized her eminence by the world. Only a few get a distant glimpse of her greatness but in it none responds to her. No Aryan prince comes forward to be the partner in her high task. It looks as though she is a matchless poet with herself as his lonely poem. She is a composer of the song of sunbright reality waiting for the flute-player to sing it. If she were a goddess in a shrine no priest would dare enter into it and wave the lamp of adoration around her. Her radiance makes her solitary and alone. None dares to claim her.

IV: 3 The Call to the Quest

This becomes a matter of concern for Savitri's father. Although there are songs of birds and flowers in the palace garden, and the winds are happy, the ancient longing remains yet unfulfilled. But Aswapati the Yogi hears other sounds in the depth of his silent heart. The inaudible promptings of Nature bring to him deeper messages. Not only that. He sees the secret divinity ready to emerge from the soul of Savitri. Behind her life is concealed the life that is to be. Perhaps man has not established contact with his inner being and possibly he understands not what eternity through her speaks to him. Yet that acquiescent attitude cannot be for his good and he must come out of it. There is a mighty Presence in her and she must awake to it. There must arrive to her the one who shall give voice to it. Savitri must discover him in the ways of the world. What her father tells to her reaches her with the power and authenticity of the supreme Mantra itself.

IV: 4 The Quest

But long is the quest and many-winding the path. She has to cross rivers and mountains in search of the joy she came to greet and affirm. Savitri has to take the lyric routes and has to climb the slopes of spiritual sublimity and wideness. She has to meet the urban gods and visit the secluded shrines in the forests. Driven from within, she has to follow her slow lingering road. Where she is going to be led of that she has no knowledge; but she has the certitude that an invisible magnet of love is drawing her to the destined place. It is in the Land of Tapasya that Man and Nature can awake to their eminent reality. Not the crowded cities of mind but god-listening silences of the woods can give to the spirit its wonder of deathlessness. Presently, when the sun is bright in the summer sky, she comes to a grove from where she need not go anywhere else.

V: 1 The Destined Meeting-Place

Designed in the sky but built upon the earth is the place where Satyavan and Savitri are to meet. It is the quintessential cosmic space and time that shaped its bright emerald reality. The breeze is fragrant and the mountains serene and the streams carry the murmuring happiness of life in their crystal flow. If fate should walk through that windswept realm of wonder and joy, it would do so only to bring the longing souls of love together. There is already the soft rustling air of expectancy and Nature is awaiting the chosen to come together. The spell of Destiny shall cast its charm on lives of the exceptional two. Unspoiled by thought and pure in its zealous gladness there burns high the incense of aspiring hope. A small pretty shrine of Shiva is guarding it against inadvertent Time. Here driven by the unknown voice of the summer arrives Satyavan to meet Savitri.

V: 2 Satyavan

Noble and erect and youthful in his Aryanhood is Satyavan. He is a Veda-knower and he has grown in companionship of nature and there is the glow of a rishi on his face. No wonder, Savitri was seeing a dream when her first glance fell on him. A miracle is done and into her life marches this alchemic splendour. An equal change takes place in Satyavan. There was until now a distressing lacuna in his life and he was looking for that which would fill it. Now it has come to him from the fortunate unknown. The joyful doors of his heart see a hidden sweetness walking into it even without knowing it. Savitri in the depth of her soul recollects her long past and recognizes the two eyes which through the ages claimed her. The presiding deity of Time took a Manvantara, an aeon, to prepare the body of Love and so has now Satyavan come to meet Savitri. Thus they arrive to discover each other and the moment stands tranquil, watching the wonder.

V: 3 Satyavan and Savitri

It is Satyavan who has to make advances and court Savitri, the sunlight who had driven itself unto him. Such things of joy and beauty he had seen but was amazed that here was she reaching him out from the heavens of happiness. He entreats her to step down from her speeding chariot and visit the creepered hermitage ready to receive her. There he read things of eternity with the eyes of the spirit. There he conversed with Nature. There he felt oneness in all that exists. But he also carried with him a sense of lamenting despondency, that body and soul have so far remained disunited. Yet he had the secret conviction that one day even the physical shall discover the true meaning of existence. It is that hope which is now getting kindled in him. Savitri shall bring about the miracle. In the union of Satyavan and Savitri shall be the union of Spirit and Matter. In the happy authenticity of such an intuition in their souls they pledge to join together. And the Gods of Nature and of the Sky shower marriage blessings on them.

VI: 1 The Word of Fate

But the incontingent love has to presently face the worldly odds, the odds of mortality. But complex is the web of Destiny and there is also the higher involvement. Narad has taken on himself an onerous task. Savitri has come to know Love, but she must also know Death. To timely impart that knowledge he hastens to Aswapati's palace and foretells about the impending doom. He comes down from his paradisal home, singing five songs that culminate in the glory and marvel about to be born on earth. He is warmly received. Savitri discloses her meeting with Satyavan; but alas it has also something ominous in it. Narad skirts it in the beginning but is persuaded to divulge the truth. In the sequel he as if tightens the grip of adverse fate by speaking about the death of Satyavan one year after the marriage. However, for Savitri's mother Malawi this is altogether unacceptable. She pleads to her, in the way of human pragmatism, to make another choice. But Savitri is firm in her resolve, maintaining that it was her soul's decision and it was not necessary for her to reverse it.

VI: 2 The Way of Fate and the Problem of Pain

The emotion-charged mother questions the way the heavenly powers toy with the human lot. She wonders how at all grief and pain

should have found a place in God's creation. Or could it be that
some disastrous power managed to mar his beautiful work? She
seems to be miffed by destiny and is reacting sharply. But Narad
reveals the sense of mystery that lies behind it. It is pain that shapes
the fiery spirit, ultimately to triumph over all obstacles. In any case,
it was man's soul that had longed for adventure and he should not
complain about it. It saw the possibility of a new creation emerging
out of ignorance and opted to participate in it. Narad asserts that
Savitri's will is fully in accord with that original wisdom and she
must be left to live in it. Satyavan's death is the spirit's exceptional
prospect and the sage convincingly as well as prophetically tells that
such an opportunity should not be squandered away. God-given is
her might and she needs no other help to carry out her work. She as
the incarnate Shakti must meet Death and transform him.

VII: 1 The Joy of Union; the Ordeal of the Foreknowledge of Death and the Heart's Grief

The royal party takes Savitri to the Shalwa forest and her heart's
desire is fulfilled. However, in the foreknowledge of Satyavan's
death the utter unknown is gaping into her future about which the
dwellers of the hermitages know the least. In the meanwhile, for the
newly wed each other's company is an unforgettable bliss. But that
happiness makes Savitri's anguish more poignant. The approaching
doom brings grief to her joy. No doubt she attends the day's household
activities with care, as would a goddess with the worldly tenderness;
yet deep in her self she remains sad. She is for a moment even
thinking of going as *sati* with her dead husband. The year is fast
coming to a close and she lives resigned to her inescapable fate. Her
daily tears only become an offering to the unsatisfied god. Yet,
gathered within, Savitri is calm. Soon would Satyavan die and she
should be prepared to meet the eventuality.

VII: 2 The Parable of the Search for the Soul

Human Savitri remains helpless in a downcast mood. But she is
attentive enough to receive the summons from her summit's being.
Her dejection itself thus becomes a yogic state; it becomes Vishad
Yoga. She is reminded of the mission she has come to accomplish.
First she should find out her soul and make in it all her actions the

actions of God. She must possess the might that conquers Death. Savitri at once obeys the directive and with that begins her occult inward journey. She witnesses the play of the subconscient forces and also the possibilities that can bring the gods down. If out of Matter and Life emerged Mind, so can a being with diviner faculties arrive here. To mould humanity in God's shape or discover a new world or create a new world are present as three alternatives and Savitri becomes the centre for the action. In the last alternative the creation established by Aswapati in the House of the Spirit shall become manifest on earth. But for any of these to happen it is essential that first the heavenly soul should be found.

VII: 3 The Entry into the Inner Countries

Savitri should discover her soul,—not for herself but for humanity. She has to step into the inner countries and meet its dread before she can make progress. There all the elemental energies swarm around her and there are the vital godheads, and the agents of the physical mind with their tenacity in ignorance, and the leviathan creatures of the fallen life, and the shady questioning beings, and the thinkers fixed in their own rigid thoughts and notions and beliefs. Savitri cuts her way through the darkness of all these dubious hues. But she also meets the bright gods who bring to her messages of greatness. She mingles happily in their company, longing yet for their spiritual light. But she is also conscious of the fact that nothing can be achieved without finding her soul. She asks for the guidance and is told that she should take up the world's highway and go all the way to its source. There she will see the occult Fire burning on a stone and the deep cavern where resides her soul. She proceeds accordingly.

VII: 4 The Triple Soul-Forces

Savitri goes deeper within and meets the three Shaktis of her soul. First is the Mother of Compassion full of suffering and divine grief, Karunamayi Mata, nursing the little spirit of man. Her task is to change this world of pain by patient work. Challenging her there stands the small life-force with its sorrow. But because of this God's labourer there is hope. The next in the inner world of Mind is the triumvirate of wisdom-love-bliss, Jnana-Prem-Anandamayi Mata.

She battles against all that thwarts progress on the road. But the fallen gods in the earth-nature oppose whatever she is trying to bring to her. She has power, yet she is unable to function here. Savitri proceeds further. If the physical world is to bear the higher descent, there must work the Mother of light-joy-peace, Prakash-Harsha-Shantimayi Mata. However, this goddess meets the opposition of an arrogant will. Savitri has to bring the absolute Wisdom, that in it might be born the divine family.

VII: 5 The Finding of the Soul

This promise can bear fruit only in the soul of Savitri. While nearing the mystic cave she experiences a strange darkness that knows the Unknown. But silent she moves on and all is the spirit's vastness. Now she is standing in front of a rock-temple with the figures of gods and goddesses carved on its walls. She sees in stone images breathing presences, deathless and divine. They are the supreme aspects climbing to Sachchidananda. Savitri crosses the tunnel through the last rock and suddenly Soul and Oversoul rush into each other. They become one. The transcendental Mother's Power, the divine Mahakundalini, floods her entire being. Lotus after dynamic lotus opens and the lower Nature becomes an instrument of the higher Nature. There is a greatening of spiritual happiness everywhere. Across death and birth the first stage of perfection is reached in life.

VII: 6 Nirvana and the Discovery of the All-Negating Absolute

But the Siddhis Savitri has attained are not sufficient. Her outer nature has yet not undergone any fundamental change and all her relationships are still human. A greater Night must therefore show her a truer Sun. She must recognize that to give a body to the Unknowable, or to burden with bliss the static Supreme, or to call down God in the human mould is premature. So she is advised to assent to emptiness, that all in her may reach the corresponding absolute. Presently she stands as a silent witness and observes the birth of thoughts; but in her spiritual immensity she does not allow these thoughts to approach her. The result is that Truth and Bliss and Love and Force are there now with her in their pristine glory. She has come to that highest Non-being which has the power to strike out the Void, revealing the One who exists unmanifest behind it. She attains formless liberation with the realization of the divine beyond the impersonal and is least concerned if she is going to disappear altogether in it or new-become the All.

VII: 7 The Discovery of the Cosmic Spirit and the Cosmic Consciousness

Beyond the Creation, beyond Sachchidananda, beyond the manifest Reality Savitri has reached the ultimate Supreme, Paratpara, the Absolute or the utter Unmanifest, the Greater Darkness of the Ancients wherefrom no return is possible. Had she merged into it it would have been a total *laya*, dissolution, and her mission would have been altogether lost. This is a delicate situation, dangerous, but a necessary experience also in her yogic pursuit, that whatever is this Nature's must disappear. By dissolution she would have crossed the realms of death; but Savitri has to enjoy immortality in birth. Her connection with this world is age-old and the little hermitage and the forest and the human life have a meaning in her transcendental realization. The Spirit of the Earth would not allow her to depart in that way. She is all that which holds death and supports the cycles of existence. The creation is a part of that Reality and the functioning its well-meant movement. Savitri has become the full divine Shakti in Space and Time.

VIII: 3 Death in the Forest

The fated day of Satyavan's death has arrived and Savitri gets ready well before the sunrise. In that auspicious hour or Bhadramuhurta she worships Durga, the Protectress of the World. Then, taking the permission from her parents-in-law she accompanies her husband to the forest where he has to go for the daily work. Even as they enjoy each other's company in the happiness of nature, Savitri is at the same time haunted by the foretold doom which will befall on Satyavan when arrives the marked moment. While Satyavan is attending to his job, of cutting the branch of a tree, he suddenly feels exhausted and there is profuse sweating as well as intense pain. He comes down from the tree and puts his head in the lap of Savitri. The noon has become dark with the presence of Yama, the God of Death. Savitri knows that Satyavan is there no more now with her.

IX: 1 Towards the Black Void

Calm and ungrieving, Savitri holds dead Satyavan in the embrace of
her soul. Presently an endless force descends in her and she is a
different person. Whatever of humanity had yet lingered in her has
now disappeared in the greatness of that death. Assuming full control
of the situation the Yogini rises to face the dreadful God. The hour
has come and she should at once take up the unfinished task of the
past. But this has to be done in the face of the opposing Spirit of the
Night. Savitri releases Satyavan from her clasp lest he should suffer
in it. His luminous spirit moves out of the body and is compelled to
proceed through the dimness of that land. Formidable Death is behind
him and he is fully under his sway. The perilous silences of the
realm shall hence keep him shut from the light of the day. But
Savitri, discarding her mortal sheaths, follows them. She is sternly
warned not to do so and is commanded to return to earth; but she
refuses.

**IX: 2 The Journey in Eternal Night and the Voice of the
Darkness**

The Yogini has transgressed the law and must pay the price for that
act of hers. She must bear infliction of the terror and accept the
denial as an incontrovertible fact. Yet her soul persists to be. Savitri
survives, but she cannot have her Satyavan back. Instead, her
exceptional daring can claim gifts from the Lord of Darkness.
Whatever Satyavan had wished while he was living, all those things
could be easily hers. His blind father would get the eyesight and also
the lost kingdom. But those gains do not mean much to Savitri.
Offended Death speaks in forbidding words. She is told that her
venturesome act should not cause the Furies to awake; instead she
should go by the wisdom shown to her by him. But Savitri is the
worshipper of Love and only by him shall she go. Indeed, in her
birth all his suns were conscient and, replies she, Death should be
fully cognizant of it. Death, however, carries in his imperial majesty
the sword of ruthless will and Savitri, once more a Wanderer in the
unending Night, travels through the unyielding vasts.

X: 1 The Dream Twilight of the Ideal

Savitri's affront cannot be taken lightly and she must be chastised for that. In fact she has committed a double sin, of harbouring spiritual superiority and of the will-to-be even in the Nihil. In that heavy and bare darkness, that terrible darkness she must atone for it. She does it and moves through the dream-ideal. There is her Satyavan, wonderful and lovely and charming. In it all pain becomes bliss. But then it could very well be that this dream-ideal was nothing but Savitri's own yearning for Satyavan, an imagination. She wanted to make him the centre of her joy and it is that which has taken this form. However, in the existence of Death even this stands at once nullified. The occult fact is that this dream-ideal cannot be safe in this mortal world. Savitri should go to the root of the matter and remove the cause of the failure. It lies in Death and therefore he must go. Indeed, he becomes negatively a touchstone for the Divinity's flawless presence in Matter.

X: 2 The Gospel of Death and Vanity of the Ideal

Earth's failure to bear the dream-ideal is tied up with the inconscient circumstance presently prevailing here. Avatar has come and Avatar has gone but nothing worthwhile has really been achieved through the ages. Savitri should therefore abandon the emotional pursuit of Satyavan's return and live in life's worldly pragmatism. Perhaps in its acceptance human suffering would not become so distressing. But she asserts that her emotion, her love is heaven-born and what she prizes is not the dream-beauty of this world; rather it is God the Fire whom she cherishes. Death ridicules it as her delusion which she must dispossess. Not only that; he is a staunch materialist and asserts that, not on Self but on Matter is founded the creation. Therefore in his theory all human love automatically gets reduced to a chemical process going on in the human body. Hence Savitri should accept the little joys that are now available to her and eventually pass into everlasting sleep of the Night.

X: 3 The Debate of Love and Death

Death's path is to lead Life to a yet deeper void. But Savitri asserts the truth which builds the worlds, worlds of the Spirit. She maintains that there is a plan behind all this in which Death himself unwittingly turns out to be a significant participator. Indeed, it was an enterprise of delight that had initiated the whole programme in the freedom of the will, even if it meant a risk or a disaster. Had this delight not been there whatever is would have collapsed. In this delight is founded true love. But for Death all this talk of glorious love is just the trickery of the Mind. Death offers several gifts to Savitri, — excepting Satyavan's life. In this deadlock finally she would be the loser and the Siddhi of her Shakti Yoga would not be achieved. Hence she must step back and in her house of meditation kindle a fire to perform the Primordial Sacrifice, Adi Yajna. She sees that there the Yajna is being performed by the Lord of the Creation and his golden Spouse and the oblations are being offered to the transcendental Reality. Savitri henceforth becomes the shaper of the events.

X: 4 The Dream Twilight of the Earthly Real

To imagine that Truth can exist on earth, that this corporeal body can house God is, according to Death, a disorientation, a deep hallucination. But for Savitri this is an indisputable reality. She is certain that Spirit and Nature can and ought to come together. Above the climbing hierarchy are ever present Truth and Love and Bliss and Beauty and she tells so to Death. The descent of that Truth can make this earthly life divine. But Death is least impressed. He insists on Savitri revealing to him her conquering power. At once a mighty transformation comes upon her. The force of Mahakundalini rushes into her and Darkness sees God's living Reality. She commands Death to release the soul of Satyavan. Death resists but he is consumed by her fire. There, waiting on the inscrutable Will, stand together Satyavan and Savitri,—but separated by a translucent wall.

XI: 1 The Eternal Day: The Soul's Choice and the Supreme Consummation

The eternal day has dawned. However, a choice has yet to be made. Savitri has vanquished Death but earth has yet to receive the boons of that victory. There are endless realms of beauty and wonder and the young couple could well live in those realms. Savitri has now to reject this Empire of Light, escape from this bright snare also. It could easily become a wide gate for disappearance into the everlasting day. But she maintains that, after all, it was to bring God down to the world on earth that they had taken birth and it cannot remain unfulfilled. Hers is the perfect affirmation of the divine in the material.

Savitri makes a choice and asks for Peace, Oneness, Power, and Joy. Identifying herself with the Will of the Supreme she prays for those boons for the good soul of the earth. 'Be it so, *tathāstu*' declares the Lord and Savitri's heart is glad. The seal of sanction is put on the incarnate Word and Superman shall wake in the mortal Man. This earthly life shall become the life divine. With the Boon held dear the two return to earth.

XII: Epilogue: The Return to Earth

The Epilogue in the Vyasa story of Savitri runs briefly as follows: Yama has departed and Savitri comes to the place where the dead body of Satyavan was lying. He regains his consciousness and makes enquiries about the terrifying figure who had dragged him with him to a strange world. Savitri mentions that it was the Ordainer of the Worlds himself who had come, but hastens to add that it was now all over. They prepare to hasten to the hermitage, as it was getting pretty dark in the night. In the meanwhile, the old parents of Satyavan get concerned for his having not yet returned to the cottage. The rishis in the forest try to dispel their apprehension with assuring words. Soon arrive Satyavan and Savitri. They are questioned as to why they were late in coming back. Satyavan tries to answer something, but he is unable to do so in proper detail. At the pleading of Gautama Savitri relates everything. She begins with the prophecy made by Narad and the purpose of her accompanying Satyavan that day to the forest. She narrates about her encounter with Yama and how she received several boons from him. The mighty God, she tells, was immensely pleased with her utterances of the Truth and, finally, among several boons granted a life of four hundred years to them. The rishis speak again and again about the extreme good fortune or *mahābhāgyam* of Savitri and depart to their cottages.

"To feel love and oneness is to live,"—that is the mantra of life in Sri Aurobindo's epic *Savitri*. In it the primordial Night, dreaming in silver peace, guards the mystic light and a greater dawn is awaited.

The Legend

The story of Savitri is an ancient story. It is both myth and pre-history. Its characters and contents are occult-spiritual. Given as a human tale, it has several connotations and is loaded with supernatural significance. In fact its symbolic nature is suggestive of the issue involved in this mortal creation, this *mrityuloka*. The issue is of a divine manifestation in the evolutionary way, evolution that has its beginning in Inconscience. There is a long spiritual tradition which carries in its experience this esoteric sense of the story.

The story appears early in the Mahabharata and is charged with the dynamism of the Dharma, the Path of Righteousness. The word *dharma* has the sense of the inner law of conduct natural to one's soul and one's spiritual build-up, one's *swabhāva*, becoming.

In the story Savitri the princess of Madra is of course the most important character. The other persons present are: Savitri's father Aswapati and mother Malawi; then, there is the heavenly sage Narad who pays a purposeful visit to Aswapati at a most crucial juncture in the life of Savitri. This happens when she is about to disclose to her parents her choice of marrying Satyavan; Satyavan, his mother Shaibya and blind father Dyumatsena, once the ruler of the Shalwa country, are staying as exiles in the forest. In the forest there are sages and learned ascetics engaged in hallowed spiritual practices, one prominent and well respected among them being the sage Gautama. Yama or the God of Death is at once frightful-dark and kind-gracious in the benignity of the Upholder of the Order of the Worlds. Princess Savitri's own birth was in response to Aswapati's prayer to the goddess Savitri. It is she who incarnated herself as his daughter in fulfilment of the exceptional boon granted to him, through her, by the Creator-Father Brahma himself. A cosmic-transcendental dimension is thus already set in the story narrated as a simple human tale belonging to the early times.

This entire paraphernalia has been pressed into the story to convey the revelatory truth of the spiritual evolution in the terrestrial scheme. Sri Aurobindo has renewed it, fixing his own yogic power into it: he has kindled the fire of his own soul in its body and in its spirit. We can thus appreciate how the story becomes both a legend and a symbol. No wonder that his elaborate presentation of the theme in the epic should focus itself on occult-supernatural actions and eventualities. Aswapati has explored the hierarchy of the worlds and found the true meaning of this creation. He has now discovered the nature of the problem and the difficulty that stands in the way. He is convinced that only if the supreme divine Power shall take birth here that this issue of mortality will be resolved.

In the Mahabharata story Aswapati is a follower of the dharma and is firmly established in the truth. He rules over his kingdom with love and has concern for its citizens. But he is issueless. Therefore with the intention of getting a son he engages himself in arduous tapasya. He retires to a forest and for eighteen years worships goddess Savitri. Pleased with his commitment to truth the goddess emerges out of the sacrificial flames and grants him the boon of a daughter. She assures him that this has the sanction of Brahma the Creator himself. In the course of time Savitri is born. She is brought up in the dignity of the tradition and soon grows into beautiful maidenhood. But because of her fiery youthful splendour no prince dares to approach her, extending his hand in marriage. For that reason Aswapati considers it perfectly in order that she should visit different lands and kingdoms in search of a young man of her choice to espouse, one endowed with qualities like her own. He tells her so.

Savitri, obeying her father, sets out on her search and travels from place to place. On her way she visits palaces and holy pilgrim centres and offers worships to the deities; also, she gives away great wealth to the learned. In the course of her journey as she passes through the green wooded regions she makes respectful obeisances to the sages and rishis staying in the sacred hermitages. It is in her sojourn at the Shalwa forest that she meets Satyavan.

Savitri, having made the choice, returns to her father's house. There as if by heavenly design is present with her father the revered sage Narad. Savitri bows down to them, touches their feet, and offers worshipful respects. Narad looks at her and makes inquiries about her. Aswapati explains to the sage that she had gone abroad in search of her life's partner and that now she must be returning after having successfully accomplished the mission. Savitri discloses that it is Satyavan whom she has chosen to marry.

But Narad, while speaking glowingly about Satyavan's qualities, also at once strikes a note of alarm, even of deep regret. He tells Aswapati about the grave nature of the choice made by his daughter. It is a matter of serious concern, he forewarns, that Savitri should have decided to take this young man for a husband. He tells them that her choice of Satyavan is an accursed choice and makes it known that one year after the marriage he is destined to die on that very day.

Savitri, however, remains firm in her resolve. She also asserts that it is her soul's choice and that she will not move away from it. Narad sees in her steadfastness something very remarkable and fully endorses her decision. He finally recommends the marriage and blesses them. Then, invoking propitious things of life and good fortune for all, he leaves the palace for his home in Paradise.

The marriage is duly solemnized. Savitri now adapts herself to the austere and simple life of the hermitage. She attends to her household tasks diligently. But, within, the virtuous woman suffers greatly. She always remembers Narad's words and feels the cruel day of Satyavan's death approaching closer. When she counts that only four days are left and after that Satyavan will be no more, she resolves to perform the difficult three-night vow, of fasting and standing at one single place through the entire period.

On the fourth day, the destined day of Satyavan's death, Savitri gets ready well before the sunrise, and lights a bright fire, and makes offerings to the gods. The parents-in-law and the rishis bless her. She requests Satyavan, as he was setting out to go to the forest for the daily work, to let her accompany him.

The young couple, hand in exultant hand, is on the way to the destined place. Satyavan shows to Savitri the tall green mountains and the sacred rivers and trees laden with flowers. In the lovely and delightful woods, with the flocks of peacocks dancing there joyously, they hear all around a soft lyrical note of cheerfulness. In that gladness the lover speaks to his beloved in honey-sweet words. But, remembering Narad's words, Savitri knows that Satyavan's life is now only in hours and he will die with the arrival of the Time-Person, *kāla-purusha*.

The hour comes and Satyavan, as he is cutting the branch of a tree, begins to feel severe pain in his limbs. Savitri immediately goes closer to him and he lies in her lap. Presently, she sees a bright Person standing in front of her. He is luminous, is imposing in his red attire, and is wearing a splendid crown over his head; it seems to her that the Sun-God himself had come there at the bright hour of that noon. His body, though dark, is lustrous in hue and through his red eyes he is looking steadily at Satyavan. He is carrying a noose in his hand which inspires great dread.

On seeing him Savitri lays aside her husband's head and stands up with folded hands. Her heart is trembling but she inquires as to who that Person is and why he was there. Yama introduces himself and tells her that Satyavan's life is over and he has come to carry away his soul. He throws the noose around it and pulls it out. Satyavan's lifeless corpse now appears very faded and unpleasant. Savitri, though afflicted with grief, follows Yama determinedly.

A little later Yama looks behind and notices her following him. He advises her to return. But Savitri refuses, insisting that she will go wherever Satyavan was being taken. She must have the soul of Satyavan back and argues extensively with Yama on fundamental issues. Her speech is perfect in thought and expression and she tells him a thing or two about the greatness of the dharma by which the creation is sustained. She asserts that the sages who live in the Truth help it grow and it is by it that the sun shines and in it the movements of Time take shape. They thus prove to be the protectors of the entire world.

Immensely pleased with the sublimity of these utterances Yama grants her boon after boon. Indeed, the more she speaks of the dharma, acceptable always in the conduct of life in every circumstance, the more the admiration of Yama for her grows. Finally, gladdened by her words of dharma, he releases the noose from around the soul of the dead. He tells her that Satyavan is now in good health and fit to return with her to do noble works on earth. Further, he grants a life of four hundred years for him to live with her. They will be engaged in performance of holy Yajnas for the welfare of the world.

After the departure of Yama and getting her husband back, Savitri comes to the place where his dead body was lying. Satyavan regains his consciousness and affectionately looks at Savitri. He feels that he is waking from some deep sleep; but then he also carries a faint

recollection of the dark-hued and terrifying figure that had dragged
him to some dreadful and unknown world. He asks Savitri whether
she knew anything about him. She tells him that it was the great
God Yama himself, the Ordainer of the Creatures, who had come
there; she, however, quickly adds that it is now all over and that he
has left the place. Satyavan wants to know more about the entire
episode. But Savitri postpones it by saying that she will narrate it
later; she points out that a thick darkness is fast enveloping them in
the forest. Then they start walking slowly back to the hermitage.
Indicating that at the bifurcation near the group of *palāsha*-trees she
should take the path leading to the north, he prompts her to quicken
the pace that they may reach home as early as possible.

At the hermitage the parents are greatly worried, that Satyavan
and Savitri have not yet returned when it had already grown so dark
in the night. But the tapasvins of the forest assuage their fear. They
pronounce that as Savitri is an exceptional woman, of virtuous
qualities, and is fixed in the dharma, and has made great progress in
her tapasya, nothing injurious can happen to Satyavan and that he is
alive. In the tranquil benign surroundings and in the manner and
movement of the dumb animals and birds they observe a secret
presence of harmony, suggesting that there is nothing which should
really cause them concern.

Then, not too long afterwards, Satyavan and Savitri reach the
hermitage and there is great jubilation amongst all present. Kindling
a bright fire they sit around it and throw a volley of questions. They
wish to know why they were late in returning when the night had
grown so dark in the jungles. Rishi Gautama expresses his eagerness
to hear everything from Savitri. She has the knowledge of all that is
far and near, that belongs to the past and to the future, and therefore
he wants to know from her the truth behind the mystery.

Savitri narrates everything in detail, right from the beginning,
how Narad foretold the impending doom of Satyavan's death, and
the reason for her undertaking the three-night vow, and of
accompanying her husband to the forest on that particular day. She
tells them that at the midday hour Yama had appeared in the forest
to take away Satyavan's soul. As he was carrying it away with him,
she too followed him and offered him high eulogies with the utterances
of the Truth. The mighty God was pleased and, beyond bound, had

become happy with her. She then narrates how she received five boons from him and how Satyavan regained his consciousness.

Next day morning the rishis, rich in splendid austerities, gather once again at Dyumatsena's hermitage and speak of the extreme good fortune of Savitri, her *mahābhāgyam*. In the course of time all the boons of Yama get fulfilled.

The Tale*

The tale of Satyavan and Savitri is recited in the Mahabharata as a story of conjugal love conquering death. But this legend is, as shown by many features of the human tale, one of the symbolic myths of the Vedic cycle. Satyavan is the soul carrying the divine truth of being within itself but descended into the grip of death and ignorance; Savitri is the Divine Word, daughter of the Sun, goddess of the supreme Truth who comes down and is born to save; Aswapati, the Lord of the Horse, her human father, is the Lord of Tapasya, the concentrated energy of spiritual endeavour that helps us to rise from the mortal to the immortal planes; Dyumatsena, Lord of the Shining Hosts, father of Satyavan, is the Divine Mind here fallen blind, losing its celestial kingdom of vision, and through that loss its kingdom of glory. Still this is not a mere allegory, the characters are not personified qualities, but incarnations or emanations of living and conscious Forces with whom we can enter into concrete touch and they take human bodies in order to help man and show him the way from his mortal state to a divine consciousness and immortal life.

---

* Sri Aurobindo's letter about the symbolic sense of the Savitri legend: *On Himself*, SABCL, Vol. 26, p. 265.

The Symbol

तत्सवितुर्वरं रूपं ज्योति: परस्य
धीमहि ।
यन्नः सत्येन दीपयेत् ॥

**Let us meditate on the most auspicious form of Savitṛ,
the Light of the Supreme
which shall illumine us with the Truth.**

This is Sri Aurobindo's Gayatri Mantra. The meditation is on the
auspicious form of the Sun, the Sun of Divine Light. The Mantra
affirms that the Light shall illumine us with the Truth. It shall illumine
all the parts of our being, even the very physical. In it shall be our
true progress. The threefold reality of Sat-Chit-Ananda shall express
itself in this creation. The purport is that even the physical shall
express the dynamic Truth.

In it we shall be immune from contingencies of Time, from the
workings of Fate. We shall be uncircumscribed by Ignorance. We
shall be free from death. Sri Aurobindo's Gayatri Mantra is different
from the traditional Gayatri Mantra given to us by Visvamitra. In
this Mantra the emphasis is on the auspicious form—*varam rūpam*.
What is implied in it is the physical transformation.

The Vedic-Upanishadic Rishis certainly had the knowledge of
the supreme Reality. They knew that in it is founded the entire
creation. But about the manifestation of the dynamic Truth in this
mortal world, in *mrityuloka*, they did not possess the necessary
working intuition. They did not know the way towards physical
transformation. Perhaps it was too early to realize it collectively
here in this death-bound world.

Now Sri Aurobindo by his intense and arduous yoga-tapasya
has prepared the required ground, made ready the *ādhār* for the
spirit's wide-ranging activities. He has made it a reality in the
evolutionary manifestation. He has invoked the supreme Grace to

incarnate herself here. She must come here and take up the work in her own hand.

The coming down of that Grace is the birth of Savitri. She alone can bring about that miracle of physical transformation. Savitri is the incarnate power who shall establish divinity in the terrestrial phenomenon.

That creative power should bring truth and light and force and bliss to the mortal world, to this creation presently governed by death. That will be her work for the fulfilment of the mortal world. Such is the significance of the esoteric birth of Savitri.

This *mrityuloka* is the great concern of Savitri. She must bring down the Truth in this world, must make that Truth dynamically operative in it. She must espouse the Truth howsoever difficult the circumstances, even in the presence of ubiquitous death.

It is to do this that Savitri comes here. She comes here as the Observer of the Vow of the Lord. She comes as *pativratā*. In the Mahabharata story of Savitri we see that she is committed to the joyous husbanding of the Truth. Perhaps the suggestion is that in an evolutionary way this mortal creation can eventually become an expression of the multifold divinity. This appears to be the true significance of the legend of Savitri. In it is the revelation of the Sun-God's transformative power.

The significance is proclaimed to us by narrating it as a story. What otherwise proves to be beyond the reach of our understanding, what is metaphysically abstuse or is too occult to grasp, that is made tangible through the medium of a household episode. The Savitri-narrative thus turns out to be a fruitful device; by it the higher truth is made to us somewhat comprehendible.

The story belongs to the early Vedic times. It is not just a social episode designed to declare moral values for the benefit of general masses. It actually enshrines the greatness of a woman's love for her husband even in the circumstance of death. It is yet something more than that,—the Triumph of Love over Death.

It is a story that depicts functionally the merit of the path of righteousness. Although it may seem to have the colouring of an ethical illustration, the story is spiritually charged. Even in the simple narrative of the Mahabharata we see a purpose behind the story, of the foundation of life based on truth. In it we notice the seeds of a brighter world taking birth.

This birth of a bright world may not be in the immediate context, but it is bound to occur in the evolutionary future. It is a new world whose birth is helped and supported by Yama, the true Yama as a possessor of gracious kindness. In it the authentic meaning, the actual significance of *mrityuloka*, becomes clearer. Yama shall thus prove to be the excellent Upholder of the Worlds. He shall then be *pitrarājastām bhagavān*, the beneficent King-Father and Lord of Creatures, as Vyasa would say.

Sri Aurobindo utilizes this legend to give mantric form to his yogic experiences and realizations, to his avataric work. His *Savitri* is therefore not only a legend and a symbol, a symbol describing the conquest of death. It is also a double autobiography. In it the pregnant Gayatri Mantra of twenty-four syllables gets expanded to fill the earthly spaces by growing itself into twenty-four thousand lines.

It has wide and far-reaching dimensions of the expressive-revelatory Word. It is that Word which shall bring noble plenitudes of divinity to this evolutionary creation. It is on this foundation that we have Sri Aurobindo's epic. Indeed, it is this which makes the poem the Epic of the Supreme.

In this Epic of the Supreme Savitri came to live with grief, to share the mortal's lot, to stay the wheels of doom, to confront death. This was the great divine task she was engaged in. For that she made the sacrifice of her suffering to the presiding Deity, surrendered herself completely to the Will of the Supreme. Indeed in it she attempted all and achieved all. In it she received the most wondrous boon of divine life on earth.

The Divine Savitri had assured Aswapati that she shall take birth as his daughter and accept the burden of the world:

> She shall bear Wisdom in her voiceless bosom,
> Strength shall be with her like a conqueror's sword
> And from her eyes the Eternal's bliss shall gaze.
> A seed shall be sown in Death's tremendous hour,
> A branch of heaven transplant to human soil;
> Nature shall overleap her mortal step;
> Fate shall be changed by an unchanging will.

Incarnate Savitri accomplished what was promised. Now the Powers of the Spirit gaze upon destiny and there is its living presence even in the commonest things. Luminous crimson seeds of God's felicity have been sown in the earthly soil. The deep red colour of the Truth-Light is indicative of the physical transformation and it is that which is symbolished here. These crimson seeds shall sprout and "this earthly life become the life divine."

Yet the question remains as to who this Savitri is. Tradition makes her an unusual princess who wins back the soul of her dead husband from the God of Death. This surely is an extraordinary event in spiritual annals of the earth. But if she is one who bears in her womb the secret birth of divinity, if she is *janani*, then definitely she cannot accept the sorrowful infliction of the death of her own child. She must become death-victorious, *mrityu-vijayini*. Her one concern is to establish immortal birth in this mortality.

Savitri is the daughter of *savitṛ* or the Sun-God who is the creator of this entire universe. This implies that we have to understand why the world is beset by the presence of Death. Why has *savitṛ* put on himself the operative veil in the pregnant circumstance of this Inconscience? Why has it to be removed by his own executive power? But then Death is also the offspring of *savitṛ* himself and therefore it becomes his concern to deal with him. For that to happen his executive power, the Sun-Word, should come as *sāvitrī*. But this happens only when the ground for her descent is well prepared here, when there is spiritual support for her birth.

When the ground is well prepared, she makes a splendid sacrifice of her transcendental divinity and accepts the evolutionary travail: she leaves her "vaster Nature" behind and works in the limits of our little terrestriality. Thus in the process of manifestation is seen the Supreme's direct involvement in the person of Savitri. Such is the correlative task cut out for her.

It was in a wondrous act of Love that the Supreme had plunged into the darkness of the Inconscience. In that way would appear out of it another creation for a worthwhile progress in the growing possibilities of the Spirit. Savitri's incarnation is for joining herself with this Love, joining in conformity with and accomplishment of the Supreme's Will. That is how the story of Savitri also becomes, through her action, the story of Love triumphing over Death. If it is through the agency of Supermind that the world came into being, it is the Supermind alone who will then bring genuine fulfilment to it in joyous glories of the Truth and Light and Force and Awareness. In it is the work of Surya-Savitri. It is that we celebrate in the Savitri-legend given to us as a great gift.

But the advent of Savitri is to be preceded by preparing well the needed occult-spiritual support; it should be able to bear the weight and majesty of her Grace. A "world's desire" has to rise to bring her birth amongst us. This is done, again, by the Supreme himself, coming here as the Son of Force. He comes here as eternal Aswapati, as the king of Madra in the Land of Tapasya. He does intense Yoga-Sadhana in the Earth-consciousness. He discerns the "wide world-failure's cause" and offers his prayer to the supreme Goddess to mission down a living form of hers. It is here that things have to happen and these can happen only through her. The Yoga-Sadhana of Aswapati is therefore to prepare the necessary base, the needed firm *ādhār* for the executive action of the omnipotent Goddess.

It is in this great symbolic background that we can also see the excellence of Sri Aurobindo's *Savitri* which is in fact the Word of Revelation adopting the fruitful form of a creative Myth, a myth that transcends the restrictive boundaries of space and time. It is a myth whose truth is being realised at every instance and on every spot. It is the Mantra of Transformation, which also implies that it is the Mantra of Manifestation. That Mantra is built into the very origin of the creation, into the stuff of things by which they acquire their validity, in turn making that myth itself an eternal reality. Be it one single resplendent word Savitri holding the Sun-God's wide infinity, or twenty-four syllables reverberating from some deep-toned womb of the omniscient Hush, or in "sessions of the triple Fire" twenty-four thousand lines spreading into the everlasting day, we have in them all present the Mantra Devata, the Goddess of Metre. We have in them all, and variously, the entrancing sweetness of her Love alone. In her dynamic action is established the supreme Truth on earth.

The birth of Savitri means the birth of a new world. This she brings about by meeting the luminous Presence behind Death and obtaining the boon of a divine life upon earth.

There is no doubt that the ancient tale of Savitri is charged with the contents of physical transformation; but then we also see that many details it has given in its swift narrative are only in a suggestive or symbolic language. Let us take an example. This pertains to Savitri's winning the singular boon of Satyavan's life from Yama. Now if we remember that the Vedic Yama is an immortal who drinks ambrosia under the *supalāsha* tree, then we at once realize as how the tale acquires its significance in the marvellous intent of this world's creation. The common name of the *supalāsha* tree is the Flame of the Forest which the Mother sees as the *Beginning of the Supramental Realisation*. It is this true Yama enjoying the ambrosial drink underneath it who gives the boon to Savitri, indicating the beginning of the supramental realization in the terrestrial process. But the story, although it is sufficiently careful to drop the necessary hints, does not go into the multiple aspects that operate in Time's dynamism. Nonetheless, the yogic vision behind it is the Vision of the Future, even if it might not spell out the means and the details to make it a reality upon earth. In fact we have in it both the symbolic and legendary aspects fused together and it is necessary that we enter into its spirit to derive full benefit from it. Add to that the mantric power that is present in Sri Aurobindo's *Savitri*, and we begin to recognise the divinity it proclaims for this mortal world, this *mrityuloka*. That is *Savitri* who gives us the Truth and the things of the Truth. Let us live in it.

Appendixes

1 Contents of *Savitri*
2 Select Bibliography

Contents of *Savitri*

Book Three
The Book of the Divine Mother

Book Six
The Book of Fate

Book Seven
The Book of Yoga

Book Eight
The Book of Death

Select Bibliography

Savitri: Sri Aurobindo
(Part One consisting of the first three Books was published in
September 1950, a few weeks before Sri Aurobindo's passing away
in December of that year. Part Two and Part Three appeared in a
single volume in May 1951. The Sri Aurobindo International
University Centre brought out the first complete edition in a single
volume in 1954; it also included the author's letters on *Savitri*. In
1972, on the occasion of Sri Aurobindo's birth centenary, *Savitri*
with letters was issued in two volumes as a part of the Sri Aurobindo
Birth Centenary Library Publication; it came as SABCL Vol. 28 and
Vol. 29. In 1986 Sri Aurobindo Archives and Research presented
the proposed corrections and revisions of *Savitri* based on the
author's several manuscripts and dictated drafts; the Revised Edition
was finalized as a single volume and issued in 1993. *Supplement to
the Revised Edition of Savitri* (1994) and *On the New Edition of
Savitri* (2000) were published by the Sri Aurobindo Ashram providing
the research findings of the Archival group. A separate volume entitled
Letters on Savitri as edited by K D Sethna was issued in 2000.)

A Talk on Savitri: The Mother
(Reported by Mona Sarkar in his *Sweet Mother—Harmonies of
Light*, 1978)

Meditations on Savitri and *About Savitri*: Huta
(Paintings based on *Savitri* under the guidance of the Mother)

Savitri: An Approach and a Study: A. B. Purani
(Sri Aurobindo Ashram, first published in 1952)

A Study of Savitri: Prema Nandakumar (First published in 1962)

Perspectives of Savitri: edited by R Y Deshpande
(The work appears in two volumes published by Aurobharati Trust
Pondicherry in 2001 and 2002; it runs into about 1400 pages and

contains more than 50 selected letters and articles written by various authors since the appearance of *Savitri* in 1950.)

Vyasa's Savitri: R Y Deshpande
(This is a verse-by-verse rendering into English of the tale of Savitri as we have in the Book of the Forest of the Mahabharata. The original Sanskrit text is also given.)

Books by the same Author

Poetry
The Rhododendron Valley	(1985)
All is Dream-Blaze	(1992)
Under the Raintree	(1994)
Paging the Unknown	(2000)
Passing Moments	(2002)
The Birth of Savitṛ	(2003)

Prose
The Ancient Tale of Savitri	(1995,1996)
Vyasa's Savitri	(1996)
"Satyavan Must Die"	(1996)
Sri Aurobindo and the New Millennium	(2000)
All Life is Yoga	(2000)
Nagin-bhai Tells Me	(2001)
The Wager of Ambrosia	(2002)
Big Science and India	(Ready for Publication)

Edited Prose
Nirodbaran: Poet and Sadhak	(1993)
Amal-Kiran: Poet and Critic	(1994)
Perspectives of Savitri I	(2000)
Perspectives of Savitri II	(2001)

N.B. *The Ancient Tale of Savitri*
has been translated into Bengali, Marathi, Tamil.